Praise for *Find Your Wealth*

Laura Moore has a rare gift for making the emotional side of money feel accessible, liberating and genuinely life-changing. She brilliantly bridges the gap between financial knowledge and financial freedom, showing us that the most transformative shift isn't in our bank account – it's in our mindset.

—**Grace Andrews**
Creator Entrepreneur

Laura has a rare gift for making you feel genuinely understood rather than lectured at; this book doesn't just change how you think about money, it changes how you feel about it.

—**Abigail Foster**
Finance Expert and Author

Find Your Wealth

Find Your Wealth

The Mind, Money, Soul Guide to Making Your Money Work for You

Laura Moore

WILEY

This edition first published 2027

Registered Office(s)

John Wiley & Sons, Inc., 111 River Street, Hoboken, NJ 07030, USA

John Wiley & Sons Ltd, New Era House, 8 Oldlands Way, Bognor Regis, West Sussex, PO22 9NQ, UK

For details of our global editorial offices, customer services and more information about Wiley products visit us at www.wiley.com.

The manufacturer's authorised representative according to the EU General Product Safety Regulation is Wiley-VCH GmbH, Boschstr. 12, 69469 Weinheim, Germany, e-mail: Product_Safety@wiley.com.

Wiley also publishes its books in a variety of electronic formats and by print-on-demand. Some content that appears in standard print versions of this book may not be available in other formats.

Library of Congress Cataloging-in-Publication Data:

Names: Moore, Laura (Personal finance educator) author
Title: Find your wealth : the mind, money, soul guide to making your money work for you / Laura Moore.
Description: Hoboken, NJ : John Wiley & Sons, Inc, 2027. | Includes index.
Identifiers: LCCN 2026024171 (print) | LCCN 2026024172 (ebook) | ISBN 9781394388103 paperback | ISBN 9781394388127 adobe pdf | ISBN 9781394388110 epub
Subjects: LCSH: Finance, Personal | Money—Psychological aspects
Classification: LCC HG179 .M66 2026 (print) | LCC HG179 (ebook) | DDC 332.024—dcundefined
LC record available at https://lccn.loc.gov/2026024171
LC ebook record available at https://lccn.loc.gov/2026024172

Cover Design: Wiley
Cover Image: Arlenta Apostrophe/stock.adobe.com

Set in 11/14 pts and Avenir LT Std by Straive, Chennai, India.
Printed and bound by CPI Group (UK) Ltd, Croydon, CR0 4YY
C9781394388127_030826

For anyone who has ever felt consumed by their relationship with money – tired of it occupying every corner of their mind, exhausted by the endless pursuit of doing the 'right thing' or uncertain about how to get where they want to be.

This is a love letter to everyone who has taken every course, read every book and attempted to follow every best practice, yet still feels frustrated by not understanding why change feels so impossibly hard, or afraid of what it means to spend, invest and enjoy.

Consider this your permission slip to explore a new way of being with money, to try something new and – most importantly – to truly start living your life. Because money was never meant to be the destination, only the vehicle that carries you there.

Contents

'Portions of this text were supported by Claude 3.5 Sonnet by Anthropic. This AI tool helped organise my ideas, provide deeper research for complex concepts, suggest alternative approaches and improve clarity throughout the writing process. All AI-generated content was carefully reviewed, edited and approved. The final analysis, conclusions and interpretations represent my views and expertise. I take full responsibility for the content and accuracy of this work'.

Preface: This Is Not Your Average Money Book

This book will not hand you an extensive checklist of must-dos, nor will it walk you through tax-efficient hacks for building wealth. If you are looking for a one-size-fits-all financial formula, you won't find that in these pages. Because money, and more importantly your relationship with it, deserves a new, more human approach.

As a qualified financial coach and soon-to-be qualified financial adviser, believe me when I say that I strongly believe in the practical side of personal finance. Building wealth is not possible without financial education and practical tools. Budgeting, tracking, saving, investing and compound interest – these are all essential topics and tools, but over the years, I've realised something important: Those tools alone are not enough.

This book is the missing link. . .

And I cannot wait for you to read it.

It is the emotional, psychological and transformational side of money that is overlooked, misunderstood and under-shared. Yet, it is the very thing that determines how you show up on your financial journey and indicates whether you can follow through on all the good financial education you have learnt. And the best thing is, it's actually simpler than you think.

My hope is that this book creates a bridge between where you are now – whether that is feeling stuck, overwhelmed, stressed or unsure how to change your current financial habits and behaviours – and where you want to be: confident, consistent and peaceful on your journey to financial freedom (whatever that looks like for you) with no judgement or shame around what 'financial era' you find yourself in.

I want this book to create financial liberation for you. No more feeling weighed down under the burden of the timelines and pressures of what it means to make and have money in today's world.

And let's be real. . . We can all relate to a feeling of financial pressure at some point in our lives.

It can be easy to feel trapped both financially and emotionally, burdened by the fear of never having enough. We live in a system that unfortunately profits from our insecurities, glorifies hustle culture and convinces us that if we just keep working harder we can finally reach a level of financial success that frees us from the drama and stress of everyday life. But this individualist approach to money, which makes us want more and more without ever fully questioning why or what it means to us, causes time to slip by unnoticed until we're too busy, too tired or too old to enjoy the money we have earned.

But there is another way.

A way of thinking about money that feels lighter, freer and more empowering. Sometimes all it takes is one new thought, one insight, one shift in perspective and suddenly everything changes.

This new way of thinking and relating to money is not one that will require you to take a sudden exit from modern society, to go live 'off-grid' in a hidden-away cottage in the woods away from civilisation, where you grow your own vegetables and collect your own rainwater and do not partake in modern-day life. Instead, it is an approach to money and wealth that is accessible, liberating and immediately available to you.

If that off-grid life genuinely lights you up, I love that for you! But it's not a path I am personally interested in taking. Even though I have completed my Duke of Edinburgh Award and I truly feel at home in the outdoors roaming around nature. . . I also love my coffee shops, city walks, buzzing day life and nightlife and being more plugged into the modern world. So that isolated life is not for me.

But that is actually the whole point here – there isn't one 'right' way to live your life or to manage and grow your money. And true wealth will look different to everyone.

A phrase that has been central in my own life is this: '*Nothing has changed, but everything is different*'.

That's the kind of transformation I really want this book to unlock for you.

There is a simpler, more peaceful and less stressful approach to money. One where money is not the final destination but rather a vehicle carrying you towards your destination: The life that you truly desire.

As wild and far-out as it might sound – especially if up until now all you have known is a sense of fear, avoidance, negativity or struggle towards money – I know this book has the possibility to free you, almost instantly, regardless of any changes to your current financial situation.

Please also know that this is not a 'money manifestation' book. I am not anti-manifestation (in fact, the total opposite!), but I'm not here to convince you that vigorously repeating money mantras in the mirror will magically pull you out of poverty, or to sell you the kind of toxic positivity that suggests you can simply *think* your way into millions of pounds without ever leaving your sofa.

I am also fully aware of the unfortunate realities we live in: the social prejudices, systemic inequalities and the capitalist structures that put some people at a disadvantage right from the very start of their lives. That cannot be ignored.

But I do believe something deeply empowering: That every single person, regardless of age, race, income or background, has the ability to change their relationship with money and feel at ease with their finances in every capacity. While our circumstances may differ, we can all free ourselves from the weight of financial stress and begin to experience money in a new, healthier, more abundant way.

So, I invite you to read this book with an open mind. I ask you to read my words with a fresh perspective on what money and wealth are and the role they can play in your life. I encourage you to approach each concept or new idea, even if it feels foreign to you, with an understanding and acceptance that you can experience money in a new way. A way where it is no longer the overwhelming focal point of your life; where it is no longer a source of stress, shame, guilt or pressure that keeps you up at night or your head stuck in the sand; instead, one where it acts a useful tool in your life.

I know this because I've experienced it myself.

Money has played a multitude of roles in my life. But over the last few years, insights into my own relationship with my thoughts about money have changed my life in profound ways. And if I can share even a fraction of what I've learnt, I know it will have a positive impact on you too.

PART I

Your Relationship with Money

Chapter 1

The Real Truth About Money

You may have heard phrases like 'money is evil', 'money makes you selfish' or 'money is stressful'. These words may even enter your mind and leave your mouth regularly.

But the real truth is that money itself is completely neutral. It is not good or bad. It is the meaning that we (as humans) choose to attach to it.

If money has been a source of anything other than ease for you up until this point in your life, then this concept may take time to sink in or wrap your head around.

At its core, money is a man-made concept, much like time. It is a symbol that represents value, and we, as a collective across the world, decided together over many centuries that money is worth something. This means money is backed by belief. It is upheld by our thoughts alone.

If every human on Earth one day woke up and suddenly chose to stop believing in the concept of money, it would become worthless overnight. It would be just paper, numbers on a screen and coins down the back of a sofa. No more valuable than a stick lying on the road. And yet in modern life, it seems to be one of the most stressful, emotional, divisive and sought-after resources in the world.

People lose sleep due to money worries. Marriages crumble under the weight of financial disagreements – money is consistently cited as one of the leading causes of divorce. The weight of financial stress becomes so overwhelming for some, that it negatively impacts mental health and, in some cases, leads to devastating outcomes. It doesn't matter if you're rich or poor, employed or retired, single or married. Money touches every single one of us. It infiltrates our daily decisions, long-term dreams, relationships, experiences and even our sense of self-worth.

For many, it holds a power that feels inescapable, like an invisible force dictating what is possible and what's not, directing the path of our lives.

Let's zoom out and remember that money was invented.

Money started with bartering, where people traded skills, goods and services. It then evolved into commodity money, where societies began swapping objects that had intrinsic value such as shells, cattle and grains. These items were accepted as a form of money because they were either rare or valuable.

Personally, I wish I had experienced living in times when pretty shells from the ocean could be used to trade. That sounds fun to me.

After that, we entered the age of metal coins, made from silver or gold – durable, portable and hard to fake. The perfect combination for trading! Paper money entered the chat in the 7th century, a game-changing alternative because it was much lighter and easier to carry than pouches full of heavy metal coins.

Could you imagine having to lug around your life savings in gold coins in your pocket? Not only would you be a very easy target for being robbed, but you would also probably spend half of your day with your trousers around your ankles.

For centuries, currencies were backed by gold, but during the Great Depression and World Wars, countries abandoned this system in an attempt to have more control over their economies.

Fast forward to the invention of 'fiat money' – money that has no intrinsic value, but is backed by government trust. This means money only holds value *because* we collectively agree that it does. Today's paper money and coins are fiat. They're not technically 'worth' anything on their own, but we accept them as legal tender.

And now, in the 2020s, we rarely use cash at all – everything is digital. We are witnessing the (seemingly unavoidable) rise of a cashless society because most money now only exists as numbers on a screen – invisible wealth stored in data on giant servers.

As you can see, money has evolved exponentially over centuries and across nations, but one thing has remained the same: Money is a tool, and its power comes from our collective belief in it.

WEALTH IS NOW SILENT

This digital evolution has fundamentally changed something about money in today's world, and it affects us all without us realising: **Financial wealth is now invisible.**

For most of human history, wealth was visible. If your neighbour had ten goats in their garden and you had only two, everyone would know who was 'wealthier'. When money was gold coins or livestock or land, you could literally see prosperity with your eyes. The rich had bigger herds and more land, so there was no way of hiding who was at the top of the financial hierarchy.

But as time went on and money became more abstract, financial wealth became both invisible and undetectable.

Nowadays the 'wealthiest' person in the room (or the person with the most money) might look completely ordinary. They might not be wearing branded clothes with logos, they might not be driving the flashiest cars and they might not be covered in diamonds. Instead, their financial wealth lives in their investment portfolios, retirement accounts and other assets – all things you cannot see because you do not carry them around with you.

Meanwhile, the person walking down the road who *looks* rich – they're draped in designer clothes, wearing a pricey watch, smelling of expensive perfume and looking all boujee – might not be financially wealthy at all. You have no real idea or true image of what their actual financial situation is. It is all smoke and mirrors.

Your automatic thought might be: '*Oh wow, they must be so wealthy. Look at all these nice things they have. I bet they are doing so well and making a lot of money!*' But really, what you are looking at is how much someone has spent, not how much they have saved or invested.

You can no longer judge someone's financial position based on how they look or what they have. It is easy to fake financial wealth. Don't get it twisted – that person you see in a designer outfit may well have a high annual salary and a well-paid job and invest wisely, creating financial returns that fund a lifestyle they can genuinely afford. Or for all you know, they could be drowning in debt, funding their lifestyle through credit cards and keeping up appearances while financially unravelling behind the scenes without a trace.

The conversation about social media and the rise of fake wealth highlights this point exactly. Your social media feed could be full of individuals with large followings flashing the cash and flying all around the world, displaying the latest gadgets and clothing. It can be easy to make assumptions about how much money they make and have.

But it only shows one small part of the picture – you could say less of a picture and more of an illusion. Cornell University research[1] by Brook Erin Duffy showed that '*most successful Instagram influencers either came from family wealth or went into debt creating the illusion*,' highlighting there is no way to actually tell just by looking at someone.

The digital age has caused wealth to become imperceptible, and social media has only amplified this, making it easier than ever to look rich instead of being rich.

---

[1]Cornell University research (https://sociallifemagazine.com/the-archive/if-i-was-a-rich-girl/).

And it can have a detrimental impact on your own finances. Credit Karma research[2] found that '*Gen Z and millennials collectively spend £400 monthly imitating Instagram stars. Furthermore, seven in ten go into debt as a result*'.

This is where it gets dangerous. When your brain fills in the gaps with assumptions, you fall into the comparison trap and start measuring your progress against an illusion of wealth. It fuels anxiety, urgency and can create a feeling of 'being behind' – even if you are objectively doing well.

Raise your hand if you have ever been personally victimised by the 'online comparison trap'. I know I certainly have! Running my business has kept me constantly online, and I've definitely noticed how easily that can spiral into comparison if I'm not intentional with my phone usage.

It can push you to spend money before you are ready, take financial shortcuts, chase a lifestyle that from the outside looks successful and make choices that do not align with you and your values or goals. Over time, this disconnect between what looks like wealth vs. what actually is wealth can erode your confidence, clarity, commitment and long-term security. This is rather insidious if you are not aware of it.

---

[2]Credit Karma research (https://www.creditkarma.com/about/commentary/gen-z-and-millennials-financially-irresponsible-era-is-over-as-many-adopt-no-buy-financial-trend).

In a world where wealth is now silent, learning to find your own version of wealth is absolutely key to long-term fulfilment.

Personally, I have come to realise that I care far more about how safe, fulfilled and financially secure I feel on the inside than how my life appears on the outside. *Feeling* wealthy matters more to me than *looking* wealthy ever could.

And I really hope by the end of this book, you will feel the same way too.

THE DIFFERENCE BETWEEN MONEY AND WEALTH

Money and wealth are two very different things, yet we often use the terms interchangeably – and that's where people can get confused.

Money is tangible. It's the asset you can hold, count and exchange for value. It pays your bills, funds your holidays and sits in your bank account as numbers on a screen. Money is practical, measurable and finite.

To me personally, money means freedom. It gives you options and choices. It operates as something that can open doors and create possibilities. Money is what you HAVE.

But wealth is so much greater than that.

Wealth is expansive, fulfilling and connected to all areas of your life – not just money or finances. It's bigger and broader than just financial wealth because *true wealth* cannot be measured by a bank balance alone.

Wealth is your peace of mind – the ability to sleep soundly at night without anxiety gnawing at you. It is your zest for life, your vitality and physical well-being, the energy you wake up with each morning and the life force that flows through you. You can find it in your relationships – the people who love you, support you and challenge you to grow. It is found in all areas of your health. It shows up in the quality of your daily choices and habits, your routines, your connection to yourself and your greater purpose, and the small moments that compound into a life well-lived.

You can have a lot of money without having true wealth. You can be financially wealthy on paper and rich in assets and still feel empty inside, exhausted every day or disconnected from yourself and the world. And conversely, you can experience wealth even if your bank account isn't overflowing with money. True wealth can be achieved through meaningful work, deep relationships, good health and a sense of purpose.

In 2025, I went through one of the toughest financial years of my life, and yet paradoxically, I ended the year feeling the most wealthy I've ever felt: I was happy, healthy and peaceful. I did not feel this way *because* of having less money but in spite of it.

Money (or financial wealth) is what you HAVE. True wealth is what you CREATE.

Money can and does absolutely play a role in building your wealth, but it is not the whole picture. It is not the only indicator of how wealthy you feel. Money is a tool that can support your wealth – buying you time, experiences, security and freedom – but it cannot replace the other pillars of a truly wealthy life.

ARE YOU HAPPIER WITH MORE MONEY?

The burning, age-old question that crosses everyone's mind! A question I am often asked and one I love to answer.

> 'The more money you have, the happier you'll be, right?'

There is a common assumption that more money automatically equals more happiness, but the argument is so much deeper than simply comparing how much money you have with how happy you feel.

The answer is not as black and white as: *Yes, it makes you happy*, or *no, it does not.*

First of all, across the world, there are extremely sad rich people and very happy poor people – highlighting that money cannot be the only factor in happiness.

From my own experience of travelling to many different countries and experiencing different cultures, I have seen with my own eyes and felt the truth of this sentiment.

However, this holds true beyond just anecdotes and personal experiences. Many studies from around the globe comparing wealth and happiness have resulted in similar findings.

Despite being one of the wealthiest nations, the United States ranks third globally for the burden of mental and behavioural disorders, according to the World Health Organization. And the United Kingdom currently ranks only 23rd in global happiness rankings despite being one of the world's wealthiest countries.

On the flip side, research tells an equally compelling story about happiness in middle- and lower-income communities. In 2025, Harvard's Global Flourishing Study surveyed 22 countries across the globe and found something remarkable. A nation that ranks low on the wealth scale is Indonesia, yet it has the highest 'flourishing' score, while Japan had the lowest despite being a very wealthy nation.

Researchers of this study wrote: '*Most of the countries that reported high overall composite flourishing may not have been rich in economic terms, but they tended to be rich in friendships, marriages, and community involvement*'.

This pattern holds true when we look at what actually predicts happiness across cultures.

The Harvard Study of Adult Development, which followed participants for 85 years, found that those who maintained warm relationships lived longer and happier lives, while those who were isolated often died earlier.

In the World Value Survey, which included 120,000 respondents from 74 nations, researchers found that closeness to community was the best predictor of happiness, even after taking into account income. Social connections, it turns out, matter as much as – if not more than – money when it comes to life satisfaction.

Therapists who work with the ultra-wealthy report that clients struggle with profound isolation and trust issues, never certain if people like them for who they are or what they have. Their relationships often become transactional, defined by what they can provide rather than who they are. Basically, they have so much personal wealth and could do absolutely anything they desired in life because money is no object. Yet, they struggle to connect with people, and their relationships often feel empty and one-sided.

Think about *The Wolf of Wall Street*, a film based on the true story of a man named Jordan Belfort, a man making millions of dollars a month in his twenties who could indulge in the things many people dream of: mansions, yachts, private jets and everything money could buy. And yet, he was completely empty inside, filling the void with drugs, sex and increasingly reckless behaviour because the money itself satisfied nothing.

In the end, despite all his wealth, he loses everything that actually matters: his family, his freedom and his physical health.

Material possessions and a never-ending flow of money cannot protect you from the consequences of aimlessly chasing money without values or purpose.

He is a perfect example of how money does not automatically make you happy, especially when you make money the goal instead of understanding what you actually want money *for*.

It also highlights the importance of beautiful relationships over money.

For me personally, I know I would rather be sitting on a sofa, laughing and connecting with my best friends in a rented house and enjoying a home-cooked meal than partying on a yacht in the Bahamas alone because I have no friends to invite.

Don't get me wrong, I love laughing at my own jokes, but the richness of true connection is priceless.

Happiness and Your Income

There is a study often quoted in personal finance circles that you may have heard of: '*Happiness plateaus at an income of $75,000 a year*'.

This research originated from a 2010 study by Nobel Prize-winning researchers Daniel Kahneman and Angus Deaton, who surveyed over 450,000 Americans and found that emotional well-being increased with income, but only up to about $75,000. After inflation, this amount is approximately a $100,000 salary in today's economy. In the United Kingdom, converted into pounds sterling, this salary is approximately £75,000.

Beyond that specific income point, they found that more money didn't make people happier.

Suddenly this finding became absolute gospel with people citing it in TED talks, self-help books and countless articles about the pursuit of wealth. If you scroll back on my social media far enough, I've probably quoted it too!

But this study did not show the full picture.

In 2021, researcher Matthew Killingsworth challenged this finding with a new study showing that happiness *doesn't* plateau at $75,000. In fact, for most people, happiness continues to rise with income, even well beyond earning six figures.

So, you might read this and think: '*HA Laura, I knew it! People ARE happier with more money*', but there is more to it.

These two researchers then decided to team up for a new study to figure out whose study was correct. In 2023, Kahneman and Killingsworth published a joint study and their results showed something interesting.

For the unhappiest people, the income vs. happiness plateau is real. Those who were already deeply unhappy – those dealing with grief, clinical depression, chronic stress or existential dissatisfaction – money only helps up to a certain point. Earning a $100,000 salary was where the positive effect of income comes to a halt.

Basically, it says: Money cannot 'fix' what is already 'broken' inside.

If you're already rich and you're miserable, more money won't make you any less miserable. It might buy some temporary relief, distraction or comfort, but money itself won't solve the root issue.

However, if you're generally content, optimistic and emotionally healthy, then more money will likely add to your quality of life.

It makes sense that when your overall wellbeing situation is in a good place, more money can absolutely enhance your life.

This is why the conversation around chasing money vs. finding your wealth is key.

If you're chasing money to find happiness, fill a void, prove your worth or escape your problems. . . more money won't save you because you're already viewing everything in life through a negative lens.

Researcher Matthew Killingsworth said: '*For very poor people, money clearly helps a lot. But if you have a decent income and you're still miserable, the source of your misery probably isn't something money can fix'*.

This is something I have experienced for myself.

In my mid-to-late twenties, I was financially at my wealthiest (on paper). My pension pot was growing; my savings were flourishing with over £25,000 and counting; I had just begun my investment journey; I had no outstanding debt; and my stable job was providing me with £40,000 a year plus commission on top. I was miles ahead of the average 20-something-year-old in terms of money.

The freedom and independence of living with two of my best friends, Fran and Beth, was euphoric. Our little duplex flat in Bermondsey was home to endless laughs and many fun traditions. To me, living with your friends feels like a rite of passage. I remember our mornings consisting of '*landing meetings*' where all three of us would stand in the doorways of our bedrooms to share the gossip from the day before and dance to girly pop songs.

But over time, once I had settled into my new home and everything became familiar, my money continued to grow, but my sense of purpose decreased. I really began to struggle with my mental and physical health.

The longer I stayed in my full-time job, the more disconnected I felt.

Every night, sleep was a struggle. Insomnia drained my health. Chronic shoulder pain consumed me. I was crying constantly and felt completely lost . . . Cue the quarter life crisis!

Many people would envy my position – a lot of money, an extremely supportive employer who let me work from home (long before it was normalised by COVID), a high salary and a position in a company that offered the potential for significant growth.

My old boss, who is still a very good friend of mine, Kieron, is one of the reasons I run my business today. He saw something in me when I was 18 years old applying to work for him, whilst all my other friends were working part-time jobs and studying for their degrees. I learnt so much about growing a business working under his wing: from making money, sales and pitching, data and analytics, managing people. . . the list goes on.

But after nearly nine years at the company (by the time I quit), all the stuff that sounded amazing on paper was not enough on its own.

My purpose was non-existent. After ditching my dream of becoming an actress a few years prior, I was now in career limbo, with no idea where to head next. I received regular promotions and pay rises; my sales bonuses would fly in every month, but they had no lasting impact on my happiness. Instead, I found myself constantly questioning and doubting everything about myself and my life.

If more money equalled happiness, I *should* have been the happiest at that point in my life. Yet, my personal experience from this turbulent time in my life reflects how income is only one small contender in the game of life.

Comparing Two Clients

If you're still thinking, *'Sorry Laura, but if someone has more money than me, then obviously they're going to be happier. I know I would be happier with more money. . .'* – let me share a real-life example.

I had two very different one-to-one financial coaching clients:

One was a 54-year-old venture capitalist earning £250,000 per year. The other was a 23-year-old on a £27,000 salary working a 9–5 job.

The first came to me stressed, riddled with anxiety and suffering sleepless nights about money. With expensive overheads, pressure to maintain and escalate his lifestyle crept in and his high income no longer felt exciting – it was an insomnia-inducing burden.

The younger client saved over £10,000 and came eager to learn about investing. She felt excited, hopeful and energised by her financial goals. Her relationship with money was positive: Calm, aware that regardless of her current income, she had the power to build her dream life. Her wealth grew slowly but sustainably, one intentional choice at a time.

A stark contrast between the two.

As you can see, it's not about how much you make, and it's not always about how much you keep. It is more about how you think and feel about what you have and therefore what that means about you and your life. That's the difference.

So yes, of course, more money can be wonderful for many reasons. I say this without shame. I plan to be financially wealthy, and I am always open to making more. More money is useful: You have *more* stability, freedom, experiences, options, security and choices.

But money is just one part of the wealth equation – it's not the *reason* you're happier.

You can still experience happiness (and a range of other positive and enjoyable emotions) at this very moment without having a lot of money.

One of my favourite phrases is: '*Everywhere you go, there you are*'. You can never run away from yourself. Your own inner world accompanies you everywhere. Yes, you can travel to far-away countries where the sun shines brighter and things feel lighter. . . where problems seem to melt away. But your problems haven't gone anywhere.

You're simply looking at your problems in a more light-hearted, detached way. When you look in the mirror, whether it's in your home in the United Kingdom or in a villa mirror in Bali. . . it's still the same *you* staring back (but maybe with a more tanned face than before!).

You can apply this to money. **More money won't just automatically rid you of all your problems.** And, with the same mindset, more money just creates new, different problems.

So, instead, you must change the way you're choosing to look at it.

The expectation that money will provide you with all the lasting happiness you need actually creates problems for yourself. You are setting yourself up for disappointment.

It reminds me of a scene from the movie *Bridesmaids* (2011), when Annie is being kicked out of first class:

The flight attendant: *'You have 3 seconds to get back to your seat ma'am'.*

Annie: *'You're setting me up for a loss'.*

In conclusion, more money does not make you happier. When you focus on creating your own wealth – nurturing your inner world, improving your health, strengthening relationships, finding your purpose, connecting with community and making time for rest and fun – you create a better foundation for happiness to thrive. And from this place, when money does come, you actually have the capacity to enjoy it. Sounds like a win-win to me!

CAN MONEY BUY YOU TIME?

Money, on its own, will never make you whole. The research is clear, but what money can do is buy you 'time': time to rest, reflect, ask the bigger questions, grieve, breathe and be.

Time itself is finite. Once a minute, hour, day has passed. . . you cannot get it back.

Money cannot buy you back the time already spent in survival mode, the seasons sacrificed to work stress or the moments lost to living life on autopilot. . . that time is gone and no amount of wealth can reclaim it.

What lies ahead is still yours to shape, though.

Financial wealth *can* buy you time and space from here on out. It can buy you the breathing room that being in survival mode doesn't allow for, and the stillness in which something so much deeper can emerge. Growth, creativity and self-discovery are available to all of us, but they thrive with a foundation of safety.

Money itself does not provide you with that growth, but it can create ideal conditions and capacity to ask: *'Who am I, really? Who do I want to become? What do I need to process right now? What mark am I leaving on the world?'*

Once I had a 1:1 client in her thirties who'd been through a rough few years – a series of unfortunate events had followed her around like a bad smell. Every day she felt exhausted, heavy and disconnected from herself.

During our work together, she made a choice that scared her but felt right: to take a short unpaid sabbatical from work using the money she saved up. She rested, read, meditated, tried new hobbies and listened to her body. She did things that lit her soul up or soothed her.

And after a few weeks she felt like a new person. Not just because she had rested from work, but because she had given herself the space to process everything that had happened. Even though nothing had changed about her past, she could look at everything from a more relaxed point of view, assess her role and emotional reactions and identify what was or wasn't in her control.

By the end, the money had gone but returning to work felt easier than expected. Her fresh perspective, renewed energy and clarity about what she wanted were all achieved through letting money provide time and space.

Money does not hand you growth, but it can create the conditions in which internal growth becomes possible. And that personal growth helps you create your true wealth, in all areas.

Similar to confidence: The universe doesn't hand you confidence on a plate. Instead, it provides opportunities for you to make a new choice that builds confidence – the moment someone asks for your opinion in a meeting, an invitation to share your story publicly or eye contact with a hot stranger in a coffee shop.

I am a big believer in going up to people and giving out your number, instead of watching them walk out without ever finding out their name. What's the worst that could happen?

Confidence grows with action; the universe simply creates the chance for you to try. And money is the same. It cannot buy you back time, but it can allow you to use your time differently.

However, having a lot of money doesn't automatically mean you're taking those opportunities.

I once went on a date with a very wealthy guy – he made his financial status very clear to me. One thing I noticed was his inability to control his own emotional reactions. Cue the ick! As a 'successful' man in his thirties, I was kind of grossed out by his behaviour: rude to our waitress, very close-minded and irritated during a discussion about children, and nasty about his ex-girlfriend (immediate red flag!).

All I could think was: '*You might have financial wealth, but you do not have emotional wealth*'.

Emotional intelligence – true self-awareness, the ability to recognise and regulate your emotions and reactions, to treat people with dignity and empathy and to look inwards instead of constantly projecting outwards – is worth infinitely more than anything sitting in your bank account.

Money can aid the process and open the door to self-actualisation, but you still have to choose to walk through it.

MOVING FORWARD

Throughout this book, you will identify what *your* version of wealth is and feel confident in your ability to create it in your life. Not society's version of wealth or your parents' version. Not what Instagram tells you wealth should be. But to find *your* wealth. Because once you're clear on what wealth means to you and how to create it, everything changes.

The impact on your life of finding your wealth will be greater than any bank balance or income can offer you.

Your financial decisions become easier, your stress instantly decreases and your sense of purpose feels clearer and stronger. And suddenly, money stops being the end goal. It stops being your source of anxiety and worry, the reason you wake up in the morning or the obstacle to living your happiest, healthiest and wealthiest life.

Money becomes the vehicle to something far more meaningful.

The meaning you assign to money is one of the greatest predictors of your financial success and your peace of mind. So, if you are wondering, '*Well, how do I actually choose the meaning I give it? How do I rewrite this blueprint? How do I actually improve my relationship with money?*'

You do it by changing your relationship to your thoughts about money (or as I like to call it – your money mindset).

Think of your money mindset like building a house from scratch.

You can fill that house with beautiful artwork and furniture, paint the walls in stunning colours and design every room to perfection. But imagine you build that house on unstable ground. You choose to build it on a pile of mud. . . it doesn't matter how beautiful or well-thought-out the interior is – eventually, the foundation will give way, the structure will become unsafe and no amount of redecorating will fix it.

Your money mindset is that foundation.

The interior represents financial knowledge you accumulate or any practical financial tools such as budgets and spreadsheets, savings accounts or cash flow models. You can have all the knowledge and tools in the world. . . but if your foundation is built on restrictive thinking: '*I'll never have enough*', or '*Money is too hard for me to make or understand*', or an identity that makes you believe you are not worthy or capable of having and growing money, your thoughts will sabotage every financial effort you make. And you will never find peace of mind with your money.

So the question isn't just *what* you are building. Nor is it about the contents inside of the house. . . The important question is what foundation are you building on?

Chapter 2

Your Money Mindset

Money *means* something different to each and every person around the world. . .

For some, it represents freedom: of choice, opportunity and options. For others, it symbolises safety, security and stability. To some, it's an amazing tool for spontaneity, adventure, experience or generosity. And for others, it represents status, achievement or validation. There are countless meanings money can hold.

What's important to understand is this: **None of those meanings live in money itself.**

Money doesn't *contain* freedom, fear, worth, safety or failure. The meaning money holds is created by how you are thinking about it in the present moment – often by taking past experiences and unconsciously layering them onto what you see today.

This is where your *money mindset* comes in.

Your money mindset isn't one single belief or story or narrative. It's the ongoing relationship you have to your thinking about money – the familiar interpretations, assumptions and conclusions your mind reaches again and again over time. And your relationship to these thoughts you have about money shapes your current financial reality.

The way you think about money determines how you feel about it.

How you feel about money influences how you behave with it.

And your repeated behaviours shape the outcomes you experience.

Over time, this is how your thinking creates your reality.

That's why two people can look at the same amount of money and live in completely different financial realities.

Let's take two people, both with £5,000 saved:

> **Person A** with £5,000 thinks: '*That's not enough. I'm so behind. Everyone else has so much more saved than me. I'm a failure. What is the point in even trying?*'
>
> **Person B** with £5,000 thinks: '*Wow, that's more than I've ever had! How exciting. I cannot wait until I have £10,000 saved*'.

Two people with objectively the same amount of money in their savings account, but their thoughts about their saved money are completely different.

They are both making a different meaning out of what they have saved. That meaning directly determines whether someone feels calm or panicked, empowered or frozen and what they then do next.

Let me share another example of how this plays out in real life:

Let's say you went to a house party with a friend *(shout out to house parties, they were the best of times as a teenager, am I right?)*.

Imagine a woman of your age comes up to you both. She introduces herself, joins in your conversation, shares a story about herself and the work she does, and you spend 30 minutes chatting away.

As she walks away you think in your head: '*Aww, what a lovely woman, she seems so sweet! And what an interesting job, I must get her details so I can connect with her*'.

But your friend out loud says to you: '*Oh god, she was so annoying, what a show-off. I hope we don't get stuck with her again!*'

You both experienced the exact same situation, with the same woman, yet you had two completely different experiences of her.

The meaning you make out of anything in life is the experience you will have.

This is why the people who struggle the most with money aren't always the ones with the lowest income or the least amount in the bank.

Throughout my many years as a Financial Coach, I've worked with people from all walks of life and financial situations, yet I see the same patterns play out again and again. Those who feel constantly stressed and anxious about money have typically assigned it a meaning that feels suffocating: Money equals survival, money equals self-worth and money equals control (or the painful lack of it).

Meanwhile, those who experience financial ease – regardless of their bank balance – tend to view money rather differently. To them, it's a tool, a resource, an energy or even a game worth playing. It is the vehicle that takes them to their end destination, not the end destination itself. This allows them to experience life to its fullest and to embody their wealthiest self no matter their net worth or how much money they're making.

The meaning you give money, whether you're aware of it or not, becomes the invisible blueprint for how you earn, spend, save and invest. It shapes whether you feel abundant or stuck, or calm or constantly braced for impact.

So if you ever find yourself wondering why you *say* you want to be 'good with money', wealthy or financially free, but your actions don't line up. . .

If you've tried changing budgets, strategies or habits and nothing sticks, or if you feel overwhelmed, frustrated or confused by your own financial behaviour. . .

Your relationship to your thinking about money will almost always explain the gap between intention and action.

The hard part is acknowledging the meaning you've given money.

The freeing part is realising that this meaning isn't fixed or unchangeable.

The fun part is creating a new meaning to have a different experience with money.

THE INHERITANCE NO ONE TALKS ABOUT

When you hear the word *inheritance*, you probably think of money, property or assets passed down through family.

But the inheritance that shapes most people's financial lives has nothing to do with material possessions.

It is psychological: This inheritance is the *money stories* you absorbed, the emotional tone around money you grew up with, the attitudes, fears and assumptions you inherited long before you had any say in the matter.

Your money mindset was formed at an early age, long before you opened your first bank account, earned your first penny or made a financial decision independently.

It was influenced by what you experienced growing up and the way money was talked about in your home: by moments of scarcity or generosity, or by conflict, tension, ease or relief. Even in households where money was never openly discussed, the silence itself communicated something. It was also shaped by your place in society, the culture or religion you were born into, and the narratives you were fed through the media and other people around you.

Over time, your mind did something very human: It tried to make sense of all of it. It innocently created meaning out of all of these money-related experiences.

I became aware of my own money mindset during my financial coaching training in 2022. For the first time, I could hear my own money stories clearly and see how deeply they were affecting not just my finances but also my career and health.

My biggest insight came from exploring my seemingly 'unachievable' dream of quitting my job and going all in on my business. My thinking was relentless: '*I need more money saved. I don't think I know enough yet. No one will pay for my services. I don't think I can make money without an employer*'. The list went on.

From a psychological point of view, it can be interesting to understand the science and mechanics of the human brain.

We have something called the Reticular Activating System (RAS) that acts as a filtering system in our mind – it sifts and sorts through millions of pieces of data, determining your experience every second of the day. It becomes hyper-aware of what you feed it – it sorts and organises your outside world based on what you value and what you believe.

For example, an expecting parent who is preparing for parenthood will be more likely to immediately spot all the shops with baby clothes and toys. Yet someone who works in tech and has a real interest in gadgets will be more likely to spot the shops selling the latest technology, completely dismissing anything baby-related. It is not an active conscious process, but it happens nonetheless.

The RAS brings your attention to what you deem to be important.

It also filters the world based on your goals and what you want to achieve.

The RAS acts like a radar, detecting data to help you identify and achieve a goal – bringing things, situations and experiences into your reality. For example, let's say you are in the market for a new car. You have your heart set on a pink Range Rover, so your brain will go to work and you will suddenly start noticing all the pink Range Rovers on the road. It is not that there are more of them than before, but you now notice them where previously you may not have seen them at all.

As Dr Robert Sapolsky puts it, '*The brain is a survival organ, not a happiness organ*'. It searches for evidence to confirm its thinking in an attempt to keep you safe and alive.

When you operate from a place of abundance – focused on all the good things already in your life, thinking thoughts of expansive and hopeful nature – your mind will bring forth opportunities, connecting you with people, places and situations that move you towards your goals.

'*When you focus on the good, there is more good to focus on*'. This phrase encapsulates how the act of practicing gratitude really does have a positive impact on your reality.

But when you operate from a place of fear, your mind will see limitations – it will show you everything you don't have, focusing on what you lack and what everyone else has that you do not. It shines a light on your mistakes, downfalls, pitfalls and problems.

My mind would replay every failed sales call I'd had whilst conveniently overlooking the clients who had already paid me. It searched for evidence to confirm what I was already believing, trying to keep me 'safe' by building a strong case for why I shouldn't leave my job. My sense of what was possible narrowed, even as I stayed in something that looked stable from the outside. And yet, emotionally I was anything but!

The functioning of your brain, and therefore the quality of your life, is controlled via your thinking and your relationship to those thoughts.

Let me share an example of how thought creates experience: Have you ever been in a situation where you think a friend or a partner is annoyed with you?

You haven't heard from them for a full day and you start spiralling.

Your thoughts kick in: '*Oh, normally I get replies to my messages straight away. And usually they like my Instagram posts, but they didn't today. . . that is unusual, something must be wrong*'.

Your brain starts searching for evidence to prove the theory of your thought, and before you know it, you start believing a made-up story. No real evidence to prove what you are thinking is true, but your thoughts run wild: '*I must have done something to upset them, this is so out of character. What could I have done?*'

These thoughts start to create an emotion in your body: You feel anxious, overwhelmed and worried. Suddenly you are in full-on panic mode.

These emotions are uncomfortable, and they then create a physiological response: You feel nauseous, sick to your stomach, you get a headache, your chest tightens and your breath quickens.

From this state you have created, you start strategising, and action follows: Maybe you text them apologising (for something you are not even sure you have done) and checking in to ask if everything is okay. Maybe you go to the kitchen and eat a chocolate bar to make yourself feel better even though you just had dinner and you are full. Maybe you go on ASOS and start shopping to distract yourself altogether.

Then suddenly, you get a text from them: '*Oh hey, so sorry for the late reply! Work has been crazy. How are you? Can't wait to see you this weekend! I miss you!*'

And in that moment, your brain goes: '*OMG, told you they were fine. I knew they were fine with you. Why did you freak out? That is embarrassing!*'

Suddenly, the mood you were in changes, the emotion seems to shift and you feel fine again.

Nothing was different from moment to moment except your thinking around the situation.

The objective truth was that the person in question was simply busy, caught up in their day. But you had one thought – '*I think they might be annoyed*' – and you RAN WITH IT. So fast you might not have even noticed it happening and how you spiralled.

Your thinking about the situation created your feeling in that moment. And your feelings influenced your behaviour. Acting in alignment with our emotions can be an unconscious process, and it can run your life if you do not understand the nature of thought and feeling.

But understanding how you work as a human can be undeniably helpful, especially when it comes to your money. Once you see how meaning is being created – moment by moment – you're no longer at the mercy of it. And from there, a different financial future becomes possible.

From a deeper understanding of the mind, you learn that feelings don't come from money or circumstances – they come from thinking. We don't *feel* our bank balance. We feel our thoughts *about* our bank balance. Behaviours and emotions are simply moment-to-moment feedback from our thinking, letting us know whether our mind is in a calm or pressured state.

This is why no amount of external change can guarantee an internal feeling. Because the feeling isn't coming from the circumstance. It's coming from the thought.

So, let's see how the psychological inheritance gets passed down to us and where it derives from.

Childhood: Your Foundational Years

Starting in your childhood, expanding in your teenage years and carried throughout your adult life, your mind has a library of thousands of stories and beliefs, and you are checking them out daily without even realising it, digesting them as the truth.

As a young person, you learn not only from language but from energy and non-verbal cues too, taking in everything around you to be important truthful information that you 'need' to store and use later down the line in order to survive as a human.

Imagine you were born with a pair of glasses without any lenses (kind of a creepy visual but go with me here. . .).

Every time you saw, heard or felt something, you absorbed it like a little sponge. Each experience acts as a little piece of glass filling out your empty frame until you have a stained-glass style pair of sunglasses. This becomes the lens through which you view the world in relation to money. It is personal to you, but it can be distorted.

Now imagine how freeing it would be smashing the lenses to see clearly. . . or maybe you could just take the glasses off to see the truth of your present reality. Either way, these glasses were your safety precaution for life and served a purpose up until now, but they give you a blurred vision about your financial reality.

These experiences include, but are not limited to, how your parents talk about money and the energy behind the conversation, and whether they were calm or charged with tension. Witnessing how your caregivers reacted to financial situations such as bills, bonuses, losses, etc. Being praised or shamed for wanting and asking for things. Hearing phrases like '*money doesn't grow on trees*' or '*we cannot afford that*' or '*I want never gets*'.

When I reflect on my upbringing, I have vivid memories of the role money played in our life as a family. My dad was a self-employed tradesman – always at work, and yet we never had much money.

All the uncomfortable situations that happened throughout my childhood made me join the dots between what I experienced, why it was happening and what that meant about me and money.

My experience as a child: Money was sparse, we never had enough money as a family and money was a source of stress.

The meaning I made: *Making and holding onto money is hard, especially if you work for yourself.*

This thinking was tightly woven into every action I took, every choice I made about spending and every decision about how I earned money.

Society, Culture and Religion

Childhood isn't the only source that feeds into our money mindset. We also absorb beliefs from the world around us – narratives that are passed down through.

The society you were born into: I love to compare the United Kingdom to America. The United Kingdom is home to '*don't get too big for your boots*' energy. There is often discomfort around openly discussing money or ambition. We are taught it is taboo to ask someone how much their material possessions cost or what salary your colleagues earn (often resulting in disciplinary action in many corporations).

Studies even show that people in the United Kingdom would rather talk about their sex lives than their financial situation. . . if that doesn't tell you what you need to know, then I don't know what will!

Yet, in the United States, hustle culture celebrates visible success and self-made wealth. It is not hard to find a conference where a speaker is on stage, raving about their million-dollar milestone and referencing the American Dream to get people on their feet, hooting and hollering. These societal attitudes seep into how we view making, keeping and talking about money.

The culture you were born into: There are micro- and macro-cultures that carry unspoken rules about money. We often absorb them unconsciously, shaped by a desire to fit in or avoid being cast aside.

For example, Western cultures tend to take an individualistic approach to money. The attitude of '*it's every person for themselves*' causes people to hoard wealth and make choices about their money that grow their own personal financial wealth, sometimes at the expense of others.

Eastern cultures, however, often have a more collectivist approach, where financial success is tied to family responsibility and community support. Both have their strengths and shadows, and both have an impact on our money mindset.

The religion you were born into: In Islam, money is a medium of exchange with no intrinsic value – it's meant to flow and serve. In some interpretations of Christianity, there is a famous quote: '*No one can serve two masters. . . You cannot serve both God and money*'. – Matthew 6:24, reflecting a belief that money becomes dangerous when it turns into a source of authority, safety or identity. And in spiritual communities, there is an underlying narrative that charging for your services is somehow 'unspiritual', keeping many healers, coaches and creatives stuck in financial struggle.

Gender narratives: Across much of the world, women's access to money is a relatively recent development. In the United Kingdom, women could only open their own bank accounts and apply for mortgages independently in the 1970s and 1980s. In many countries, financial autonomy arrived even later – and in some places, it is still restricted today. This exclusion from financial conversations, decision-making and wealth-building has left a legacy of gender bias, whether you like to admit it or not. Many women today, and many in my online community, still feel like money isn't for them or struggle with guilt and anxiety around earning, charging or negotiating.

One of my favourite pieces of research was conducted by Anne Boden, the founder of Starling Bank, as part of her #MakeMoneyEqual campaign.

After analysing 300 financial articles from men's and women's magazines, her team found that 65% of articles aimed at women defined them as 'splurgers' – excessive spenders who need to limit and restrict their shopping habits. Meanwhile, 70% of articles aimed at men positioned financial success as making them 'more of a man', focusing on investment strategies, wealth-building and earning more.

As Anne puts it: '*Language is separating us into spenders and earners, into the frivolous and the empowered. Men are advised on investment strategies, whereas women are told to stop splurging and buy fewer shoes*'.

And beyond childhood, society, culture and religion, there are certain significant events and crises that stand out and can leave deep imprints on us. For example, a family bankruptcy, a sudden inheritance, a lottery win that changes everything, being labelled the 'rich kid' or the 'poor kid' at school, or a financial betrayal, e.g. lending money and it never being paid back.

These emotionally charged moments, traumatic events and unexpected financial situations all play a significant role in what money means to us and what it can (or can't) do.

And it is important to highlight that you do not simply become a carbon copy of the people who raised you or those around you. You do not blindly replicate everything you saw, heard or experienced growing up or throughout your younger years. But those experiences do leave a mark, and the way this shows up in your life now will look entirely different from one person to the next.

This is evident in my own family. I was raised in the same household, with the same parents, and the same environment (and objectively the same circumstances) as my sister and two brothers. Yet, as adults, we each have a remarkably different relationship with money because each of us as individuals internalised and made meaning of what happened in our own unique ways.

BELIEVING YOU CAN CHANGE

To be reading this book right now there must be a glimmer of hope inside of you that knows you're capable of change. It may not be a large glowing ball of belief the size of the sun. But perhaps the flicker of a flame or the very start of a fire. That is enough to get started.

A book I read and loved was *Mindset* by Carol Dweck where she shares the concept of a growth mindset vs. a fixed mindset.

In the book, there is a study that really struck a chord with me. In 2007, a study was conducted with seventh-grade students who were struggling academically. Students were divided into two groups. Both groups received eight sessions of study skills training including practical tools for how to study better.

But one group received something additional: They also read a single article titled 'You Can Grow Your Intelligence: New Research Shows the Brain Can Be Developed Like a Muscle'.

That was the only difference.

An article explaining that the brain is like a muscle, that it grows stronger with use and that every time they learned something new, their brain formed new connections.

The article didn't give them tips; it didn't tell them what to do and it did not give instructions on how to change. It simply explained the possibility of a different future by cultivating a growth mindset. And the results were insanely cool.

The students who only received study skills (the control group) continued to see their math grades decline throughout the year.

But the students who read the article stormed ahead and their grades rebounded. The article alone was enough to give them the understanding and the hope that they could change, regardless of their starting point. That their intelligence was not fixed and their studying efforts would pay off – even if they themselves did not deem themselves smart enough to get a good grade.

How cool is that?

The same is true with money.

Regardless of your childhood, culture and experiences and of how deeply ingrained your financial habits and behaviours feel – change is more possible and more within reach than you might expect.

You are not broken. Change does not need to take years of inner work. You do not need more budgeting tips or savings hacks, *although of course those have their place!*

What you need is a deeper understanding of how your mind works and an awareness of the meaning you are making out of money.

Hopefully this shows that your money experience is far more fluid and flexible than it feels. And the messages and methods in this book will not send you into a strict money mindset routine that you must execute daily with full commitment until you have overridden the system and created a new foundation. It is far simpler than that. When I learnt this, it was a relief.

PART II

Your Financial Eras

Chapter 3

Every Season Matters

I have a truth to share with you.

Your financial trajectory will not be linear.

Despite what you may have been told, financial growth does not follow a lovely, neat, upwards curve. It won't just increase slowly and steadily year on year: making more, saving more and growing more.

Instead, your financial journey will ebb and flow. . .

Sometimes your money might go up and down like a pogo stick.

Other times it might swing left to right like a methodical pendulum.

It might even unrhythmically flip-flop about like a fish out of water.

It is ever-changing. And it is not to be feared.

The sooner you can understand, accept and surrender to this fact, the easier and more enjoyable your life will be.

SUMMER IS NOT THE ONLY IMPORTANT SEASON

Much like the cyclical nature of life, humans too go through seasons.

If you live in the United Kingdom, you know we experience every season in full force. We rotate through the crisp, hopeful energy of spring; into the warm and buzzing freedom of summer; into the cosy, golden calm of autumn; followed by the slog of the cold, dark winter.

And clearly from my own descriptions, you can tell: I am not a winter girl. I am a summer girl until the day I die.

I honestly wish I could bask in the heat and frolic around in the sun 24/7. But for as long as I live in England, that is just not possible, sadly. The geographic location of this country means our climate provides us with the full range of seasons.

When the days get darker and the air turns cold, your body naturally wants to slow down. You sleep for longer, you withdraw, rest and hibernation vibes kick in. Do not mistake this for laziness. Your internal system is telling you: Please restore now so that you can bloom later.

> 'Nature never rushes, yet everything gets done'.
> —*Lao Tzu*

If you try to fight this season, forcing yourself to stay in 'summer energy' during the winter months, your body will push back at some point. Your immune system gets overloaded, you're low on vitamin D, exhaustion takes over and suddenly you're bed-bound with the flu. Refusing to give yourself the break you need and deserve results in this unwelcome break being forced upon you and against your will.

Throughout my life, I've often struggled to feel comfortable stopping to rest. I would push throughout the winter months, in an attempt to be productive and efficient. I treated myself like a mechanical being, stuck on a loop and wrapped up in a barrage of beliefs. And the end result was never enjoyable.

Sometimes I would be sick and in bed for weeks; I'd feel burnt out, creatively blocked and mentally tired. I would be exhausted in every area of my life.

All because I identified with the thinking that wanted to fight against rest. It showed up in many different ways:

- **Fear of falling behind:** I worried that if I slowed down, everyone else would keep going and I would lose momentum in my career and progression towards my goal. Rest felt like regression, like I was willingly and carelessly letting opportunities slip through my fingers while others capitalised on them. Rest meant something about my connection to my goals.
- **The productivity myth:** An internalised idea that my worth is tied to my output. If I wasn't producing, achieving or visibly progressing, I would unknowingly question my own value. The belief that my worthiness to rest had to be earned. That rest was indulgent, a luxury and made me lazy, or even selfish because there's always more I 'should' be doing.
- **Loss of identity:** Busyness, for as long as I can remember, was a part of who I am. And slowing down meant confronting uncomfortable questions: '*Who am I when I'm not constantly doing?*'
- **Comparison and social proof:** Social media created the illusion that everyone else had an endless source of energy, so if I was not keeping pace or matching their output, something must be wrong with me.
- **The 'just push through it' mentality:** We've been taught that discomfort is weakness, and that resilience means powering through regardless of how we feel. Acknowledging our need for rest feels like admitting defeat or a lack of discipline.

ATTACHING PRODUCTIVITY TO YOUR IDENTITY

I was a very active and energetic child, and it followed me into adulthood, but I didn't realise or like to admit that sometimes my battery needed charging. I convinced myself that I had an endless supply of energy but in truth, my inability to rest was the cause of stress and sickness on many occasions.

My first job at 16 gave me a taste of swapping my time for money, and 10 years after that, I worked multiple jobs, always stretching myself thin because I was desperate to provide myself with financial security.

During the two years of my A-Levels at school, I worked every weekend as a Team Leader at Argos with my mum as my manager, and I also cleaned the school every weekday evening. I stayed behind after the school day ended and cleaned the very classrooms my friends and I had been studying in, just hours before.

When I left school and landed my first full-time job working 9–5 at a marketing agency, I also had multiple other jobs: I waitressed at a bar and restaurant, and for weddings and private events. And I had an acting agent, and so sometimes booked commercials – if you search hard enough on the Internet, you can find my TV debut when I appeared in a short advert where I'm dressed as a chav – and I used to do medical role-play. Some would say I was the side hustle queen.

By the time I started my own business at 27, the classic entrepreneurial lifestyle had fully gripped me, and for the first few years, I worked every second of every day. I was constantly on my phone, using social media, networking, going to events and serving clients.

I attached my entire identity to my busyness. It felt like it was all I knew.

I know I'm not alone in this. Conversations with friends and people in my community constantly circle back to this theme; everyone seems to have wrestled with the same struggle at some point in life. The sheer volume of content out there proves it: articles, podcasts and videos exploring this from every conceivable angle.

On one side, you have the glorification of hustle culture, the relentless push to work harder and be more productive. On the other side, there's a growing movement dedicated to dismantling the belief that rest is weakness, offering mindset shifts and practical strategies to help us actually stop, breathe and let ourselves rest without guilt.

In 2022, I moved into the house I currently live in. We nicknamed it 'The Womb' because it metaphorically acts just like that: People say they leave the house feeling rebirthed. It exudes beautiful feminine energy, and it has certainly been a sanctuary for me, fostering much of my own personal growth over the handful of years I have lived there.

Each evening or weekend, Jo and Ju (two of my besties who I live with) would sit down on the sofa to either watch TV or wind down from the day. But I always had ants in my pants. I remember not feeling physically able to 'relax', unable to stop and sit still, always thinking about what I needed to do next or what I *should* be doing instead of taking a little break.

As the months went on, and I settled into my new home environment, my housemates helped me realise something that I always knew deep down but struggled to accept: My productivity and my self-worth were intertwined.

WE'RE HUMANS, NOT ROBOTS

You may have seen or heard of the beautiful but harrowing robotic art installation: *Can't Help Myself* by two Chinese artists, Sun Yuan and Peng Yu. The piece became a viral symbol of burnout and the unsustainability of pushing without rest. It featured an industrial robotic arm programmed to contain a thick, blood-red liquid within a specific area on the gallery floor. But the fluid would keep spreading, and the robot would desperately try to sweep it back. Its efforts were endless, unforgiving and futile.

Seeing this living piece of art broke my heart, and I actually cried when I saw a video of it online. The poor little robot never took a break, and over the years its movements became slow and laboured. What began as an energetic, almost dance-like performance, inevitably deteriorated into something very tragic – a visceral metaphor for exhaustion, the illusion of control and the cost of relentless labour.

It is the pressure to constantly perform, to keep everything contained and to never stop working even when the task itself is unwinnable, regardless of how you feel and what your body yearns for: a period of rest.

But luckily the world is waking up, and we are coming round to the idea that rest is important and non-negotiable.

Choosing to honour each season of your life or your finances is not a weakness.

In fact, flowing with nature and moving with the seasons is what creates a beautiful and peaceful existence – times of doing and times of being. When you allow yourself to slow down, you naturally create reserves for more energy, life force and excitement for the next season. I like to see it as the pulling back of the arrow before it launches into the air again.

Rest is essential for so many reasons, and yet we attach so much meaning to it.

Your 'winter' does not need to *mean* anything. Putting a negative label on this season only leads to frustration, stagnation and resistance that transforms into ailments. You will feel completely deflated if during this period your mind is racing with thoughts of '*Oh I should be out partying, I shouldn't be in so much, I need to leave the house more, why can't I get up at 5 am anymore to exercise? I'm not productive enough at the moment, I have so much to achieve in my business, why do I look so unwell?*'. It removes all of the enjoyment of the slow and restful season.

The resistance to the slower times in your life only creates more stress, noise and worry.

Well, the same applies to your money. . .

Nothing blooms all year round.

So, why do you expect your finances to be in constant bloom? How can you expect your finances to be constantly growing, blooming and bursting with life when we know we shouldn't ask that of ourselves?

What we don't hear often enough in the world of personal finance is that 'not every season of your life will or can be a saving or investing era'. It is not a failure; it's simply life.

Naturally, we all will transition in and out of different 'financial eras' – times where we spend more money, times where we prioritise saving, seasons of investing in ourselves or the future and periods where our finances aren't even on our minds, and we are just surviving as best we can.

So, measuring yourself against an unattainable ideal of financial perfection, and resisting the natural evolution of your financial era, is a guaranteed way to burn out and block your own peace and cause your own suffering.

Just like leaving an event without going to the toilet first, knowing you have a long journey home: Failure is inevitable. And no one wants to feel stressed about money AND have wet knickers.

Many things can change your financial situation: the career path you take, the stability of your income, big life milestones such as travelling the world, buying a property, setting up a business or having a family.

Then, there are also unfortunate events that occur beyond our control such as a death in the family, an unexpected illness, a messy divorce or sudden redundancy – all of these things directly impact your money.

Some are predictable, some unavoidable and some even life-changing.

The bottom line is living life costs you money.

And pretending otherwise or ignoring this truth can have a detrimental impact on you, your health and the quality of your life. It stops you from ever creating true wealth.

In many years of my career, I have noticed that people find it extremely hard to admit this to themselves. This is especially true in an age of social media clickbait and Instagram highlight reels: Sometimes financial growth won't be your priority, but it's important to really know and believe that it is okay.

Unfortunately, in a capitalist world, the dominant narrative of personal finance conveniently ignores this truth. It sells you a robot-like vision of success: Always earn more, never dip into savings and build wealth with unbroken consistency. In the words of Kylie Minogue: 'More, more moreeeeee'.

This dream is packaged up in a pretty little pink bow and sold to us as superior to all other routes. It is *shit rolled in glitter*, and I'm not buying it!

Because we are not robots (surprise): We are human – real humans with feelings, thoughts, desires, fears, different perspectives and experiences. We are messy, complex, emotional, intuitive and our financial journeys are human too. Yet this polished, perfect-looking path – the idea that we should prioritise steady, unwavering wealth over everything else – is a myth.

It sounds ideal on paper, but it's not realistic for anyone.

On paper, it also sounds *ideal* to have your life all figured out in your twenties: to journal and meditate daily, always skip caffeine, avoid texting your ex. . . but is that realistic? I think most of us have had a different experience pre- and post-twenties, winging it daily with coffee and a prayer. And that's okay.

The expectation to always be in your best financial shape is one that no human can *realistically* uphold.

And honestly, it's not something we should even aspire to. Life is not built for constant upwards motion and pretending this is possible only sets us up to feel like we're failing when we're simply being human.

THE IMPERFECTION OF PERFECTION

If you have ever felt a sense of unease when facing decisions that have the potential to slow down your financial growth, make things feel stagnant or even make you feel like you're going backwards, I feel you. You are not alone. As an adult in the 21st century, it is understandable if you feel stressed when your financial life isn't on this perfect upwards financial trajectory.

Especially so if you grew up in the era of the Internet, the age of Tumblr (RIP my favourite platform), MySpace, Facebook, Instagram, TikTok, YouTube. . . everywhere you look, it feels like someone is hitting life goals and financial milestones. It makes you think '*Why do they all have a secret sauce that I don't seem to have the recipe for?*'. It feels like a secret club that only you have been left out of.

But something I have learnt is that there is no secret sauce and perfection does not exist.

And I know this because I live this. In spite of my job as a coach, creator and speaker in the finance space. . . I still have had an absolute roller coaster of a journey with my finances. And I would be lying if I said I haven't had times when I look at other people around me (other FinFluencers or financial educators) and start to question if I am doing something wrong.

Thoughts of perfectionism slip in quietly and show up as an uncomfortable forceful pressure: *Do more, be better and get it right.*

For most of my life, I actually believed there was a flawless version of me, my life and my finances waiting somewhere. And if I just tried a little harder, I'd reach it and finally feel safe, secure and at peace.

I'd ride off into the sunset, having 'perfected' life and live happily ever after. The determining factor of whether this became a reality was down to me and my efforts.

But I was so wrong.

Those feelings of safety, security and peace don't come *after* perfection or *because of* perfection. You can experience them right now without anything being flawless. You can experience financial peace in this exact moment as you read this book. The irony is that when you let imperfection exist and move through your seasons with ease, those feelings you're so desperate to find begin to rise naturally.

Paradoxically, the more you loosen the grip around an ideal image of how your finances 'should' progress in order to feel calm and safe, the more you increase your chances of experiencing these feelings.

The idea of something being perfect is usually a coping mechanism designed to make yourself work harder, to self-sabotage your situation and to ensure you don't take your foot off the gas of working towards your dream so that you don't become complacent. . .

But can you imagine how it would feel to acknowledge, respect and own the financial eras you have been in, and the one you are in right now?

Chapter 4

The Danger of Rejecting Your Current Financial Era

You know what they say: 'Expectation is the thief of joy'.

Expectations ruin everything.

An expectation is simply a thought in your mind. It is a mental image of how you believe something should unfold – the keyword being *should*. And like any thought that pops up in your mind, you have the power to accept it or reject it.

THE DIFFERENCE BETWEEN HOPE AND EXPECTATION

The difficult part is that expectations often masquerade as something helpful. We tell ourselves we are being prepared, or setting standards, or protecting ourselves from disappointment, or ensuring that we have the best possible outcome of an event or situation. But there is a crucial difference between expectation and hope. Understanding the two can change everything for you.

Hope is light and open-handed. Hope says '*Oh I would LOVE for this to go well, I hope it does!*', but it leaves all the room and space for reality to surprise you. Hope acts as a buoy, keeping you afloat in times of uncertainty or despair. Most importantly, it does not demand or *expect* a specific outcome; instead, it holds space for possibility. It allows you to move towards something you would want without gripping it so tightly that it crushes you completely in the process. It says '*this would be nice, but if it doesn't happen, I'll still be okay*'.

Expectation, on the other hand, is heavy and closed off. Expectation says '*this must happen this way or I will be disappointed, upset and not okay*'. It is a fixed mental script of how things should go. But the issue is that when reality deviates from this made-up image in your mind, even slightly, it feels like personal betrayal – like the world is against you!

Unlike hope – which keeps you buoyant – expectations become like a heavy rock tied around your ankle, dragging you straight to the bottom of the emotional ocean (or as I like to call it – the Em-Ocean. . . get it?).

When you set your expectations high and anchor onto them like your life depends on them, you create a wall between yourself and your reality. You stop seeing what is and only see what isn't, focused on what failed to match the picture in your head.

But there is something more insidious about expectations: They are rooted in the belief that you can predict and control how your life unfolds to the minute detail and that you make meaning out of everything that doesn't match your expectations. Trying to impose order on an inherently unpredictable existence is the quickest and easiest way to a miserable life.

Whether you like it or not, life – and your finances – do not owe you anything. And they certainly don't owe you the script you chose to write for yourself. These scripts of expectation create noise in your mind, a constant mental comparison between 'what should be' and 'what is'. This noise is deafening at times and completely drowns out your ability to experience and appreciate what is actually happening in front of you – regardless of whether you choose to label it as good or bad.

Hope, in contrast, creates so much space that it allows you to wish for something without demanding that the universe comply with your orders. Hope does not collapse when reality takes a different shape, but it chooses to adapt, breathe and accept by saying '*this may not have gone the way I hoped, but that is okay; I can still find meaning or joy or peace or gratitude or a lesson here*'.

EXPECTATIONS CREATE JUDGEMENT

One example of how this shows up in our reality is going on holiday.

We put so much pressure on ourselves for the holiday to unfold perfectly as planned. You have saved up the money, booked to visit a new destination, planned every detail in your carefully thought-out itinerary and you imagine yourself completely relaxed, making the best memories.

But when you arrive, little things go 'wrong': The hotel room isn't as nice as the photos, it rains the day you'd planned to go to the beach, the restaurant you were buzzing about trying is fully booked or you get sunburnt on the first day.

And suddenly you are in a bad mood, disappointed and stressed out, scrolling your phone instead of being present. Not because the holiday itself is bad, but because it is not matching or living up to the version you built in your mind.

Meanwhile, your partner or your friend who you are there with is having a lovely time – enjoying the local food, laughing at the unexpected moments and making the best of it all.

Your holiday was not ruined, but it simply couldn't live up to the pressure of the perfection you put on it. This idea, that things must go a certain way and match your expectation in order for you to relax and enjoy yourself, is made up. Yet, if you'd let it unfold naturally, without gripping onto expectations, you would've enjoyed it so much more.

Back in 2024, I went on holiday with three of my girlies (Nina, Big Eloise and Little Eloise) to Sorrento in Italy. The trip was iconic. We loved it so much that we made a group decision to go back again to the same location the following year in 2025.

Both years I had an equally amazing time but for different reasons. They were two completely different experiences, with new inside jokes and freshly created memories, but in the same location with the same people. Instead of expecting the holiday to copy or even beat the previous year, I let the return trip unfold naturally.

The lack of expectations allowed me to be more present and enjoy the trip to its fullest.

When your financial reality doesn't meet the standards you have set, you judge yourself – and that judgement can be absolutely paralysing.

You may begin to tell yourself:

- *'I should've saved more by now'.*
- *'Everyone around me is ahead, I'm falling behind'.*
- *'If I quit this high-paying job to chase my dream, people will think I'm irresponsible'.*
- *'Why isn't my income growing like I thought it would?'*
- *'I cannot believe I've spent all this money!'*

These thoughts not only cause an unsettled and ungrounded feeling inside of us, but more often than not they also lead us to self-sabotage and lose trust in our own financial power. It is the place where most people get stuck. Not always because their bank balance is objectively terrible, but because of the story they're telling themselves about their money and/or the financial era they are in.

Can you notice and feel the difference?

The problem is not your financial situation, but the stories you are telling yourself about your financial situation, and the meaning you are making out of it.

So what are you telling yourself about the financial era you are in right now?

Do you feel like the tides are turning, a new one is ready to enter the room? Maybe you have been on a spending hype recently, and you're feeling the natural pull to lean back into cutting back a bit and saving a bit more.

Maybe you have been saving so much and sticking so well to your budget and you are feeling yourself swaying over into wanting to have some adventure, and it's time to spend and have some fun.

Bring awareness to how you think about your current financial era. Are you judging or are you simply reflecting?

When judgement enters the room, it leaves no space for life's twists and turns. It silences intuition and blocks joy. It stops you from taking life-changing opportunities simply because they cost money. It can make you ignore your body when it needs rest, and it can make you fear taking risks even when the reward could transform your life.

If you constantly judge the financial era you are in, you remain trapped in your own mind and not in tune with life's moments and opportunities.

There is no need for extra judgement or to be hard on ourselves if you have been judging yourself. . . We all do it, it happens! But when the judgement does fall away because you have seen something new about your situation, the relief tastes so sweet.

Chapter 5

The Sweet Relief of Non-Judgement

Birthday celebrations have always been a great marker of where my energy is at.

I experienced the sweet relief of non-judgement on my 32nd birthday in October 2025.

I spent my birthday alone – this was an intentional choice, and I love a solo day. The plan was to get a massage, take myself out for a yummy brunch, visit the bookshop and then spend the afternoon in a coffee shop journalling and reflecting, before my friends came over for a takeaway in the evening. *A DREAMY DAY in my opinion.* And I felt super excited to celebrate and was accepting of my choices to keep it low-key.

For context, the last two birthdays I'd had, I partied hard for my celebrations.

My 30th birthday holds a special place in my heart. I threw the most iconic house party. It is where my desire to start DJing was born. Hours were spent singing and dancing to all the 1990s and 2000s girly classics, and there really is no better feeling than screaming at the top of your lungs with your best mates to songs such as 'Unwritten' by Natasha Bedingfield and 'Foundations' by Kate Nash.

And to top it off, as a lifelong sweet treat hater and never being able to eat my own birthday cake, my housemates presented me with a 'non-cake': a savoury alternative, a giant sandwich covered in cream cheese to look like a cake; it was the perfect way to begin my thirties. Nothing could top it. . .

Then 31 rolled around, and I didn't want to throw a giant party. I was too worried that I would spend the whole time comparing parties. So instead, I celebrated in other ways. . . I'd not long returned from a trip to Ibiza, and I had a full-on birthday month full of small celebrations with different friends from different groups.

So then, when my 32nd birthday arrived, I toyed with the idea of throwing a big party again.

But that was not the energy I was in, and I didn't judge myself for wanting to enjoy another year around the sun in a more chill way.

I felt a pull to be more introspective. I craved a relaxed and slow day. Birthdays always make me super reflective, and I love to think back over the last 12 months: What I learnt, what I am letting go of, the highs and lows, and the person I was a year ago vs. now.

For me, 2025 had been my most challenging, turbulent and testing year, and I like the thought of my birthday being an energetic reset, cleaning the slate for the next year ahead. I wanted to have a good day with the 'perfect plan' I'd created. . .

But guess what? The day absolutely did not start as planned.

LETTING GO OF EXPECTATIONS

I woke up on my 32nd birthday in an insane amount of pain because of a frozen muscle in my neck, so I had to swap my luxurious massage for an appointment with my osteopath. This threw a spanner in the works.

As a Libra sun sign and a previous people-pleaser, I haven't always been the best at making decisions;

whilst my decision-making skills have improved immensely over the years – sometimes I still fall victim to old patterns of thinking!

I fell into a battle in my mind, bouncing around a million different questions: '*Do I go to the gym first or straight to the osteopath? It would be nice to have a swim and sauna on my birthday. . . oh wait, but do I even have time before my appointment? I guess I could just have a sauna and head straight into town. Well, should I eat first? But I don't want to ruin my appetite for brunch. . . Maybe a snack? But what snack!*'

This went on for about an hour (no exaggeration), and I stood paralysed in my bedroom, overwhelmed by choice.

As I felt the frustration set in, something clicked in me and I made a decision. . . I was proud of myself. But what proceeded in the following hours was a string of unfortunate events: Someone knocked a row of Lime bikes that fell like dominoes onto me and crushed my leg. Ouch. I missed out on breakfast at one of my favourite brunch places, London Grind, by literally five minutes as it changed to the lunch menu; I broke the zip on my favourite coat; I spilled super-hot coffee on my leggings – just to name a few.

> 'I can't believe all of this is happening to me. . . AND ON MY BIRTHDAY! Is this a sick joke?'

I could feel myself wanting to throw a tantrum in the middle of the street, and I nearly burst into tears – one thing after another. All I could think was '*what does this mean?*'

> 'Does this mean that my 32nd year is doomed? I've already just had the hardest year of my life, and I can't do another one. Is this a bad omen?'

Then I stopped and actually started to laugh out loud.

Even though my day was not going exactly to plan, it did not need to put me in a bad mood for the rest of the day. I could choose to laugh at the things that have happened, take them for what they are and let them be. **Every moment is a doorway into a new emotional experience.**

A birthday doesn't define a life, and it definitely doesn't decide how the next year will go. It is just an imperfect day in a bigger story of my life.

My judgement fell away, and I had an amazing rest of the day. . ..

My osteopath worked his magic and relieved me of my back pain. I then stumbled across a new café that I had never been to before and had the most delicious brunch, and I ended up making friends with the chef. They gave me my matcha latte for free as a birthday gift. My journalling session was so moving, and I felt an overwhelming sense of peace and presence. I cried in the coffee shop.

So, yes, I did end up crying on my birthday, but for the best reason – out of gratitude, not frustration.

I'm an emotional girl, and when the tears come, they cannot be stopped!

Old Laura – the one who had not yet learnt about the transient nature of thought and emotion, the one who yearned for every moment to be perfect, the one who self-abandoned to people-please those around her, the one who was yet to go through her biggest life-altering experiences – would have led herself unknowingly into a low mood for the remainder of my birthday from hanging on to intense judgement, and all those wonderful things would have been missed or underappreciated.

And we do the exact same thing with our money.

CREATING A RICHER LIFE

We set huge expectations, often without even noticing – about how things *should* go. Stories about what financial 'success' is supposed to look like get built up and latched on to. We create mental timelines, imaginary milestones and ideal scenarios.

Then, when reality doesn't align perfectly with this image in our head, when there's a dip in income, an unexpected expense or we simply feel behind in comparison to others. . . we immediately judge it or ourselves, deciding that something has 'gone wrong'.

And just like my birthday, that's where the suffering begins: Not in what actually happens, but in the gap between our expectations and what is.

If it seems funny that I'm comparing a bad start to my birthday to our overwhelming financial concerns, keep in mind that this is not about *what* we're judging. It's about *the fact* that we're judging at all.

Some people go through massive, objectively stressful life events – financial crises, big transitions, uncertainty in relationships and jobs, and housing circumstances – with a strange sense of calm and clarity. All because they aren't judging the experience while they're in it. They're simply allowing it to be what it is.

And then there are times people spiral over something objectively small – a late fee, an impulse purchase, or a bad day for example – and let that moment define their entire self-worth. Not because it's such a huge deal on its own, but because it has been judged and labelled as *bad*, or as a sign of failure.

Judgement distorts our view. It exaggerates, dramatises and catastrophises everything in our sight and in our mind, making everything feel heavier than it actually is or needs to be.

The irony is that sometimes we think we're being 'responsible' by being hard on ourselves, but all that happens is we make it harder to move forward in any direction.

So, focus less on the size or seriousness of the situation and more on how quickly you go into judgement. How fast or frequently your mind says '*this shouldn't be happening*' or '*I messed up*' or '*I'm behind*'.

What if nothing was wrong? What if it just *was*?

What if the same way I stopped judging how my birthday went, you could stop judging your money story and finally start rewriting it with compassion, not shame or expectation.

As Eckhart Tolle said: '***the moment that judgement stops through acceptance of what is, you are free of the mind. You have made room for love, for joy for peace***'.

The moment you stop judging your financial era and accept what is, you are free and you make room for more freedom, peace and joy in your relationship with money.

Living in a constant state of saving, investing and growing your money is simply not sustainable. While important, it can be just as damaging to our lives as it can be helpful – if it's rooted in fear or guilt, or if you are acting out of alignment, or if you are doing it because you think it is what you should be doing.

That mindset can cause you to miss out on the very experiences that make life rich, meaningful and fulfilling because the richest life is not about accumulating as much financial wealth as possible without any failures, dips or downturns.

You create a wealthy life by using your money as a tool to grow, develop and experience. And that becomes possible when you detach from the false idea that success only comes in the form of financial perfection.

Instead, you focus on cultivating a healthy relationship with money, improving your own financial knowledge, building helpful money habits, acting in alignment with your truth and trusting the seasons you are in. Learning to embrace your different financial eras creates space for financial peace and ease.

You stop fighting with where you are, so when opportunities arise that require you to use money, imagine how freeing it would be to say 'yes' or 'no' based on what truly feels right, not what fits someone else's version of financial success.

What happens if you resist the natural changes that enter your financial life? You can take things to the extreme.

Chapter 6

From Eras to Extremes

Layering judgement on top of your natural cycles will calcify a financial era into a financial extreme. When you grip tightly onto one financial identity, it becomes fused with who you are. You make it your safety, your proof of worthiness and, in most cases, your entire sense of self.

FLEXIBILITY, RIGIDITY AND INTENTION

A financial era is a season you move through with awareness and intention. You're in it but not stuck in it. The more you get to know yourself, the easier it becomes to feel when it's time to shift.

You could characterise it by flexibility (you shift when life calls for it), awareness (you know the intention behind your behaviour), ease and flow (money moves through your life in service of your needs), and trust (you believe the season will change when needed).

A financial extreme is when you remain in one financial era that began with fear, judgement or childhood conditioning. The behaviour becomes rigid, compulsive and damaging. You're no longer flowing because instead you're frozen.

This looks like rigidity (not being able to deviate from your habits even when it would serve you), compulsion (it feels like a need, not a choice), fear (either hoarding or haemorrhaging money intensely) or resistance (where you fight against any natural pull to shift).

What matters here has nothing to do with *which* era you're in (surviving, saving, spending or investing) and has everything to do with the intention behind it.

Saving 50% of your income every month can be a powerful wealth-building era if it comes from intention and alignment. But it becomes a financial extreme when it stems from fear or lack, refusal to enjoy your life or inability to spend even when you desperately need something.

Spending everything you earn because you're in a season of improving your health, transformation, creating experiences that matter or building something life-changing is a powerful investing era. But if it's compulsive, driven by avoidance or not-enoughness, then it leaves you with more stress than growth and becomes an extreme.

In both examples, the former is healthy and supportive; the latter is restrictive and damaging. The energy behind your actions is everything.

I don't believe financial extremes are inherently bad or that you're broken if you recognise yourself here. What I *do* believe is that when we take our financial hits to an extreme in either direction, it creates psychological, energetic and physical instability in our everyday existence.

CHRONIC OVERSPENDING AND CHRONIC OVERSAVING

Let's compare either end of the financial spectrum. At one end you have chronic overspending; at the other is chronic oversaving.

Chronic Overspending

One of the most commonly discussed financial issues is overspending:

- never being able to stick to a budget,
- saving or investing nothing,
- money leaving your life as soon as it enters,
- living pay cheque to pay cheque despite earning more than enough.

If you spend everything you make each month, keeping nothing for yourself or your future, you never create any financial stability or resilience. Money flows in and back out of your life so quickly that you can't harness any of the resources, options or breathing room that come with having financial reserves.

This extreme is often driven by avoidance, distraction, fear of stillness or trying to fill an internal void with external purchases. It feels pretty icky if you ask me!

Spending itself is not bad, but the ongoing impact of chronic overspending can be significant. It means you never have the financial resources or power to make real change in your life. You miss out on all the freedom that comes with having financial resources: the ability to walk away from a job or relationship that's turned toxic, the security of growing investments that protect you from financial crises, big trips that require saving or life milestones that need cash reserves.

Society would have us assume that overspending is 'the bad one' and oversaving could never be harmful. I definitely used to believe this!

Chronic Oversaving (Hoarding)

It can look like:

- saving and investing everything,
- feeling anxious or guilty spending any money on yourself,
- denying yourself experiences and joy (maybe even necessities),

- missing out on opportunities because you can't bring yourself to use your resources or money.

My money hoarding began at age 16 at my first ever job. I always felt like I was doing the right thing by saving every penny I ever made, disciplined enough to say no to many opportunities in favour of growing my personal savings – don't get me wrong, it felt amazing to create a financial safety blanket for myself so young. But at some point, the script flipped for me, and I realised that hoarding is just as damaging as overspending when the energy behind it isn't one of expansion and flow.

The energy behind this extreme is often from fear or a scarcity mindset, a feeling of no control so you aggressively control your financial flow or unworthiness ('*I don't deserve to enjoy my money*').

Saving and investing for the future is important, but when it becomes so rigid you can't shift out of the pattern even when your life is asking you to, you will never get to enjoy your money or your life. You stay on the hamster wheel of more, more, more, forever deferred gratification and forever waiting for 'enough'.

I often say '*You work too hard for your money to not ever enjoy it*'.

I also often say '*You were not put on this earth to ONLY pay bills and save all your money*'.

Read whichever one suits you because they both apply.

Chapter 7

Financial Habits Are Not Only About Financial Growth

Throughout my adult life, I have transitioned through different financial eras quite naturally – flowing through surviving, spending, saving and investing – going with life's ebbs and flows, growing my money and drawing down on it when needed, and learning incredible lessons along the way, without much judgement of myself.

Whether I knew it at the time, I often did a great job of listening to my intuition (even though I didn't even think I had one!) and following the breadcrumbs of opportunities left by the universe. I learnt to not let fear of financial ruin get in the way of the life changing experiences that shaped the woman I am today.

This is where it all began…

FROM FEAR TO INTUITION

The first time I started saving money and achieved a big financial milestone, I got stuck in a financial extreme. At 19, when I began my first and only full-time job, I was delusional enough to believe saving £15,000 was achievable, regardless of my humble beginnings and a lack of financial role models at the time. The motivation to save was fuelled by my passion for acting, but the chronic oversaving was a result of my limiting money beliefs. The fear of never having enough stopped me from ever dipping into my savings.

Desire filled up the piggy bank, but fear put a lock around it and threw away the key.

I tied my sense of self-worth to my savings and denied myself necessities in the name of career devotion. But even though my scarcity mindset created waves of stress, worry and vulnerability, there was also a positive consequence: the financial power I created for myself.

The ability to say yes or no based on what I wanted, not on what I could afford, was the first positive experience I had with money, the start of building a beautiful life using money as a tool and flowing through it.

My £15,000 in savings was initially to pay for Drama School tuition. . . Instead I spent it all in eight months travelling with two of my best friends, Beth and Emma. No regrets!

Words don't do justice to the fear I felt making the decision between two potentially life-changing opportunities: one was a dream 12 years in the making since my first ever acting class at age 10 and the other was a new dream unearthed as the adventure presented itself. It was an opportunity to see the world outside of my hometown with two of my best friends.

Money gives you choice. A lesson I learnt at 22 when I was presented with a once-in-a-lifetime opportunity; I had enough money to say no to a path that no longer felt right and to say yes to a new path.

I immediately knew the answer, and the thought of going to Australia lit me up in the most magical way – I couldn't ignore it. But that is not to say I wasn't absolutely petrified at the thought of dipping into the money I had worked so hard to save. It didn't make any sense to me at the time, but something in me knew that travelling was the right decision, regardless of all my noisy and fearful thoughts.

Guided by a wisdom that lived dormant inside of me, ready to be finally heard, I trusted that using this money would in fact give me something greater than I originally had planned, even though I did not know what that looked like.

My logical mind could not have predicted the trajectory my life took after I cast aside judgement and acted courageously and committed to the choice my intuition nudged me towards. On 2 December 2015 when I boarded the flight to Sydney, I started along a new path that led me to where I am now.

Choosing to spend all my money in eight of the most amazing months of my life gifted me many beautiful lessons that negated any judgement I had regarding no longer having money in a bank account.

I snapped out of my financial extreme of hoarding money, and the fear of not-enoughness started to fall away. Spending my money from a place of excitement and alignment led me to incredible experiences such as Scuba diving on the Great Barrier Reef and sailing around the Whitsundays. The only regret I had when I returned home was that I wished I'd stayed in Australia longer.

ALIGNING WITH HONEST GOALS

Taking a sabbatical from my 9–5 job gave me the space to slow down inside and reconnect with myself. It's clichéd, but I found (parts of) myself travelling. There was a little voice inside of me that was asking me to look at other career avenues, but it went unnoticed, cloaked under the noisy thoughts of not-enoughness.

For years, my attention was focused on the external (achieving financial 'security') so much that I ignored the internal – the part of me that no longer wanted to follow an acting career but was too scared to admit it to myself.

As I sat looking out across a beautiful lake in Sydney, I admitted to my best friend '*I don't think I want to be an actress anymore*'. My entire identity was wrapped up in this aspirational job title. I was no stranger to telling anyone I met that I wanted to be Kate Winslet in *Titanic 2* or I wanted to be in *Glee*, when asked the question '*And what do you do?*'. So much of my life had been devoted to performing, and here I was ready to give it all up.

That honest admission opened a window in a room I'd been living in my whole life. I didn't even realise how stale the air had become until fresh air came rushing in. I was unaware of how much I'd been breathing in the same recycled dreams and the same prescribed identity, all because I'd been caught up in external validation trying to feel safe and in control by working hard and saving my money. And once I felt that breeze, I couldn't pretend the window didn't exist. I found the confidence to walk away from a career I had desired for my whole life.

This Australia trip also opened the door towards a more intuitive relationship with money, and each step down this path allowed me to accept the ebb and flow of my financial journey. It became second nature to use my money as a tool throughout my twenties in whichever way life asked me to. The absence of judgement made it easy to make aligned choices and share my story online.

Upon reflection, it was less about how much I had saved or invested, and more about cultivating financial habits that supported all areas of my personal life, not only my financial growth.

I am who I am because of how I've used my money, not how much I've saved.

When I returned to the United Kingdom from Australia aged 23 in 2016 and got my old job back, I found myself back in a new financial era. The travelling fire had been lit inside of me and it was burning strong. There was a strong desire for adventure and newness, so when the opportunity arose to move to London with two of my best friends, Fran and Beth, I trusted my savings capabilities and confidently started scouting for homes to rent in South London. This time round, I was stepping into my savings era with a fresh perspective and excitement to reach my new goal of moving to London and then backpacking in South America.

There was no judgement when I started this new savings journey from scratch with £0 in my pocket, a little bit of debt, a mind full of memories and a new perspective on life. I simply started making money again and shifted my habits to create the reality

I wanted without worrying it would take too long or never happen for me. Or that my current reality was something to make meaning out of. I had no money, but I had so much more than money.

To me, what I had gained felt priceless, so I didn't question the position I found myself in; I was just ready to shift my behaviour and get my finances flowing again.

Don't get me wrong; it came with its challenges, but mostly my mind was free of doubt, confident in reaching my new savings goal. My vision board back during this time in 2018 was showered in photos of girls sunbathing, books I wanted to read and quotes saying 'GIRLBOSS' and 'WEALTHY QUEEN'. In the middle was a huge number '£20,000' in bold pink font. I leaned into the abundance of life to rebuild my money pots.

The energy behind my savings habits felt fun and easy. I still experienced life, and I made some sacrifices but not to the extent of full deprivation: I had boundaries, but there was flexibility. I worked multiple jobs and increased my income which propelled me to save 25% over my original goal of £25,000 in a few years. I left behind my old town, moved to the big city and felt excited about this next adventure!

After two years of living in London, I was preparing myself to jet set again with a carefully planned-out itinerary and travel budgeting plan, but then suddenly the whole world stopped. Chaos ensued; COVID-19 meant everyone had to stay inside and my dream of learning Spanish in Peru after hiking Machu Picchu was dead. I felt flat. With all this money, I can't experience the one thing I had saved up for over the past few years.

At the height of lockdown, I started sharing my journey online – what else was there to do?

INVESTING IN THE FUTURE

Luckily the aliveness (from the prospect of my backpacking trip) transferred into a different adventure: the start of what is my business today. I dived right in and invested in technology and equipment, business coaching and a mastermind, my financial coaching qualification and so many more things with no previous business experience, except what I had learnt in my sales job.

Being a business owner comes with a price tag. I made mistakes, spent money I didn't need to and invested in things that were a waste, but it is all part of creating a career where your time is your own. I once spent £300 on a course that felt like it was written by a six-year-old. I spent hundreds on systems that I couldn't figure out how to work or solutions that only made my life harder.

But it is important to share just how much I have also gained from starting up and running a business. Right at the start of my journey of putting myself out there online, I got one of my first invitations to be a guest on a podcast. When I spoke with the host of the show, Gaby, over FaceTime to do a chemistry test before the episode, we ended up speaking for over two hours, and a few years later, I was a bridesmaid at her wedding! A beautiful friendship was born out of a business connection. This is one example of many people who are now present in my life thanks to my business.

Extending beyond just friendship, I have been invited to the House of Commons to share my opinion and help create change to the UK school curriculum to include financial education. I have attended the Bank of England to talk directly with the Financial Conduct Authority and Advertising Standards Authority alongside my Finance Content Creator friends to discuss policy and guidelines for online education and how to protect the country from financial scams. And it was one of many other incredible opportunities to make a real impactful change.

The people I have met, the rooms I have found myself in, the transferable skills I have gained and the people I have helped as a result of starting this business are worth every penny I've spent.

As I grew my social media following sharing tips on how I saved £15,000 at the age of 19 and on changing your money mindset, I also fell into the world of investing – I actually first learnt about investing when I was on a date with a man and he couldn't believe I was holding all of my money in cash and not investing. The date did not go any further, but my curiosity about investing did.

The future of my life looked dramatically different after I learnt the concepts of investing and started building my own wealth. It was so empowering and exciting, and I wanted to share it with everyone!

Building your financial wealth comes not through saving every penny you make, but instead through investing and generating a profit through owning assets such as stocks and funds. Learning this changed the trajectory of my entire financial future. And it was a double whammy because, as I grew my own personal finances, I also learnt to become a better financial educator – teaching people about the stock market, the power of compound interest and exponential growth.

If you have never used a compound interest calculator before, you are missing out. It's this online calculator that predicts how much your investments will be in the future depending on how much you say you can afford and the % return you might expect from your portfolio. As a self-proclaimed 'spreadsheet girly' who loves numbers and maths, I geek out on this shit.

I would play around and imagine what it would be like to have a million pounds sitting in an investment account. For the first time, financial independence felt more like a reality than a pipe dream. No longer would I have to work as hard as I had been; I could finally put my money to work. The idea of freedom acted as fuel for my investing habits.

When I created my online mini-investing course for beginners that demystified the emotional and practical sides of getting started in the stock market, breaking down the jargon and helping people build confidence in becoming a successful investor, I could never have imagined the ripple effect it would create.

Through my business, I got to pass down the life-changing knowledge and real excitement that learning how to safely invest can and will change your future, regardless of your financial upbringing or background.

The universe works in wild ways, because while writing this chapter, I received an email from a previous client, Sophie, with a beautiful share: '*I did your Feel Good Investor course in November 2023 and no word of a lie, it has completely changed my life. Before I found you on Instagram, I used to cry with fear at the prospect of opening a bank account. I was financially illiterate and it fuelled my fear. Since November 2023, though, I have done a complete 180. I committed to learning about personal finance and have been investing for 2 years consistently. My fear and panic have gone. I grow in confidence all the time. And I have even found I now actually enjoy learning about personal finance!*'

The investment of my time, energy and money that I put into sharing this knowledge with my community and clients has continued to pay me emotional dividends for years. Seeing how this work impacts people on a daily basis is worth every penny and minute I have invested in being a business owner.

As I grew my own investment knowledge and continued to share online with my community, I implemented the very things that I told other people to do and added to my investments consistently and periodically over time. And it felt right and easy at the time. It wasn't forced. I loved the feeling of making money and then investing it and seeing it grow. The energy behind those habits was expansive.

This investing era flowed naturally and without judgement. I invested in my business, the stock market and my own future. I learnt a lot from it, and so did my community. I built a beautiful foundation for whatever the next section of my life was.

Each era that followed the other taught me something, and the focus was on what I was gaining, not losing.

Where I went wrong this time, though, was allowing judgement to seep in and sit at a table it had not been welcome at before. And for the first time in a long time, it left me stuck.

Chapter 8

You Are One Thought Away from Freedom

My track record shows me that all my financial eras always served me in some way when I moved through them without judgement. I always came out the other side with a new skill, a fresh perspective on life, stories I will tell for the rest of my life or something that money couldn't buy: wisdom.

I'd travelled the world and created beautiful memories; I'd learnt the skill of saving and investing; I had started a new business that was bringing me an income; I was getting ready to quit my full-time job; I'd made new friends and connections; and I had left the financial extremes behind. My acceptance of my financial journey grew healthier and stronger every year.

Yet, fast forward to 2025, at the age of 32, after having to dip into those same savings and investments, I was no longer as financially secure as I'd have preferred. For the first time, I felt crippled by overwhelming shame about my declining net worth so much so that it kept me quiet and in a behavioural cycle: I dipped into my investments, spent without intention or awareness, avoided my money and ghosted my online community with my silence around my own finances – where before I used to share so openly and confidently.

ALL ABOARD THE JUDGEMENT TRAIN

I looked at my situation through shame-coloured glasses, completely blind to the contributing factors for my financial position. For the first time, I was really judging myself for the financial era I was in.

Every day I was on a loop of thinking:

> 'How on Earth can I share online with my followers about where I am at? I am meant to be an expert on personal finance and money mindset and here I am with less in savings and investments than before. Why would they want to

listen to me?! Girl, you cannot tell people what's going on, what would they think of you? God, you're useless'.

I've always valued transparency and believed in leading by example. I never want to contribute to the online noise of inauthenticity and hide the messy parts of life. When I began this career, I didn't choose to create a pact with myself about showing up truthfully and authentically. . . the pact was written into my soul. It's part of who I am.

But I honestly felt AWFUL for a good chunk of time!

I didn't even understand it myself and all it was doing was causing so much noise in my head. I was writing a book on this topic: *'AM I MAD? Who will take me seriously? Why am I such a failure? This is so embarrassing, I am an imposter! A FRAUD!'*

The heaviness of judging my current financial era started to weigh me down. I couldn't make sense of it all. I just knew I felt icky about my money! Handcuffs on, stuck in thought-jail and believing every thought about my financial situation.

I despised how my finances 'felt', how I thought it would look to other people and the thinking I was having around my situation. The judgement train passed through the station and I jumped right on – CHOO CHOO.

I was so caught up in it that I couldn't see the bigger picture.

EXPERIENCING A BREAKTHROUGH

When I stopped focusing on finances and looked at my life as a whole, it was the best it had ever been. I was the healthiest I'd ever felt (mentally, physically and spiritually). My life was a result of how I had chosen to use my money, specifically the last two years from 30 to 32. The only thing blocking my peace at that moment was judgement.

> 'Hang on. . . Why do I shame myself for the spending that has now shaped me? How can I resent spending money when it gave me what I needed, when I needed it most? Isn't that what money is actually for? Isn't that what I have experienced time and time over?'

It was a rainy evening in the summer of 2025 that I had a HUGE insight into the evolution of my own financial relationship that changed everything.

Late one night when sleep wasn't looking promising for me, I lay on my bed in silence, letting my mind wander. . . I was feeling a bit stuck, struggling to show up online consistently and unsure about the next step to take in my business. There was something deeper that I wasn't seeing yet.

One fateful conversation with my wonderful coach and very good friend, Jessie Douglass-Smith McGraw, unlocked a beautiful breakthrough. It was probably one of the most important insights I have had when it comes to my relationship with money.

I sent her a voice note telling her how I was feeling about my life, money and business. It was the paradox of feeling the most grounded I'd ever felt before in all parts of my life, yet the least connected I'd felt to my work in the financial space and the most ashamed I'd felt about my own financial situation. My heart opened up and all the judgements I had about myself flowed out.

Her reply reminded me that THIS is what I teach. I am the embodiment of my own work and beliefs. I show people that money ebbs and flows, and my own life is a reflection of that.

She said '*you have learnt [firsthand] about what it is like to ride the ebbs and flows of life because your best practices have led you to a place in your business, financially, where you have been able to give yourself the space to grow and stretch and meet yourself where you are today as opposed to always continuing to function from what has always worked.*

You have been in the pull to evolve and go beyond your growth edge. . . but it is your own best practices around saving and investing that have allowed you to do that'.

The realisation came rushing to me. It was clear as day and completely freeing.

I wanted to do a cartwheel, down a pint and run around the room naked. But instead I stared at my bedroom ceiling for a solid ten minutes, or it could have been one hour. Who knows, all I know is I was stuck in that floating feeling that comes with an epiphany – flung from confusion to freedom in SECONDS as I floated around in a time-suspended world.

In that moment, as I began to untangle a new layer of attachment to money, I saw so clearly the stories I'd been creating and thinking I had been clinging to. I believed that my financial situation somehow reflected something bad or broken about me. The thinking that popped up said this financial era meant *more* because of what I do as a job. I linked its meaning to my work. And because I am so closely attached to my work, I then attached meaning to my worthiness.

I had been believing that my most recent financial era meant

- I was no longer qualified to share financial education.
- I would never reach the level of wealth I truly desired.
- I won't be successful and I will be rejected by everyone.

Somehow, I'd slipped into thought cycles I help others break free from. I've learnt that when you slip into old ways of thinking and you act from your busy mind, not your calm intuition, judging yourself only makes it worse.

So I sat with it for a sweet minute and without force, clarity came through.

It was like my past suddenly flashed through my head all at once. Everything felt interconnected; nothing was separate.

One thought had given me complete freedom.

Chapter 9

Wealth Helps Differently in Each Era

What is the point of having money if you cannot use it when you need it most?

The keyword is 'need' – not when you want it most, but when you really need it.

Sometimes you save money with a very clear purpose in mind and then that purpose changes. Like when my drama school fund became my Australia fund – it felt easier to accept the change in purpose for that money because it was still going towards something I valued and really wanted. Not the dream I started with, but a new one that popped up in my life.

But unfortunately, sometimes life does not give you a pivot that feels good or aligned. You might have to spend your money in crisis mode. You may need to rely on your money to keep yourself together emotionally, physically and spiritually, to support your family when they need you and to handle emergencies that do not mirror the neat and predictable events you are warned about by financial experts such as losing your job or getting sick or your washing machine breaking down.

You save for emergencies 'just in case', and when one actually happens, you hesitate. You wonder if this one 'counts' and is worthy of the money you have saved, questioning '*is it bad enough yet?*', and if you should actually wait for something worse to justify dipping into those savings.

It is like installing a fire extinguisher in your kitchen and then refusing to use it when one of the bedrooms catches fire because you are saving it for an expected fire in the kitchen – saving it for a 'real' emergency later down the line.

Life is full of unexpected twists and turns. And emergencies are not just the ones you expect. They are all the unexpected things. In the book *Same as Ever*, Morgan Housel, one of my favourite authors, writes that risk is '*what is left over after you think you've thought of everything*'. You can do your best to plan for all eventualities, but it is the ones lurking in your blind spots that are the real risks and unfortunately there is no way around this.

Since you can't predict the biggest risks, you should prepare for the unexpected rather than trying to make a perfect plan, and he says that, in financial planning, this means saving more than you think you need and taking on less debt than you can handle.

AN ERA OF FUN AND SPENDING

So what actually led me to this financial shame spiral? What happened in my life and finances?

Around my 30th birthday, I felt myself leaving an investing era and flowing into a spending era. At first, it was intentional and then it was unexpected. It started off as investing in myself and then it became a matter of survival. And the judgement was keeping me from seeing the magic in this time of my life.

Before I turned 30, I had no debt and had money saved and invested. But when I turned 31, everything changed, and the unexpected came along and it broke me open in ways I could never ever have imagined or anticipated.

The solid foundation I had set for myself was rocked: I spent all that money. At first, the spending happened in a planned and controlled way, but it turned into something so much greater that I had little control over.

Had I chosen not to spend it, telling myself it wasn't 'serious enough', I genuinely do not know where I would be right now. My money did what it needed to do – it held me when I couldn't hold myself and I am now so grateful for that.

The first few years back out into the real world after the two years of lockdown during COVID-19 were all systems go. My new career was blossoming, and my finances were growing. I had worked so hard running this business as a side hustle that I was ready to quit my day job. I was absolutely loving it, but whether I could see or admit it, I had slowly become burnt out.

I felt like my life was missing something. If you follow me online, or listen to my podcast *Mind Money Soul*, you will know that I am a girl with a lot of energy and a library of fun stories. I love live music, to go out and dance, to go to festivals and to explore. I love travelling and holidays. I am super social and I was missing that part of my life – the playful, whimsical, fun part.

So, when I turned 30 in 2023, I listened and gave myself what I needed. My body and soul were craving fun and adventure.

Upon reflection, if I were to answer honestly, I could have been more mindful with some of my spending choices. But there is no point judging myself because the year of being 30 (from the end of 2023 and throughout most of 2024), I had one of the best, most memorable and most needed times of my life. I found myself again.

Well, I should say I found a new version of myself, and I loved meeting her. The new life force that was running through me, filled up from leaning into fun and play, overflowed into my work and my business began to thrive.

All of life is interconnected – when you listen to the nudges that don't make logical sense, anything can happen. When I show up for myself in one way, life surprises me in another way. For example, you can set a boundary in a romantic relationship you have and then you find that a relationship at work sorts itself out. Loosening the grip and seriousness in life and finding my childlike play again mirrored itself in my business: Showing up felt light and fun, and opportunities were flowing.

AN ERA OF HEALTH AND SELF-DISCOVERY

During my era of fun and spending, I was not really saving or investing. I prioritised experiences that brought me back to my joy again. But I also felt it was time to seriously invest in my health. I was so fed up with yo-yo dieting, inconsistency with working out and chronic shoulder pain that wasn't fully healed.

The only constant in my life had been walking and my yoga practice. But everything else around it was scattered and forced. And for any female business owners out there, you will already know the challenges that come with our hormonal cycle, let alone health challenges on top that fog up your brain and 'cost you time' in your month.

So, alongside my year of fun, I explored naturopathy, Chinese medicine, acupuncture, osteopathy and kinesiology. Looking after my body and calming my nervous system to reduce the inflammation in my body was my priority. I had always had an interest in holistic healing, but this time it was coming from a place of curiosity and wanting to feel good in my body to experience life to its fullest. Rather than punishment or restriction, as I am sure many young women have experienced through the course of their years.

As my fun and healthy year drew to a close and I was getting ready to turn 31, I finished my last trip of the year in one of my favourite places. The real ones know that Ibiza is not just a party island, but somewhere mystical that also holds a lot of magical energy and beautiful sunset spots.

I was feeling a natural pull back into my saving era: I was ready to get my head down, lock into my business and generate an increase in my income. But then something unexpected happened. . .

AN ERA OF LOVE, LOSS AND SURVIVAL

In September 2024, the month before my 31st birthday, on a retreat in Ibiza, I met a beautiful French man, and he swept me off my feet. I entered the new year, the start of 2025, in an unexpected long-distance relationship.

It felt like I was living in a Hallmark romance movie. I went from being the girl who at 30 years old had never been in a relationship, ever, to being the 31-year-old woman who had fallen in love in Paris and spent many weekends travelling through airports or on the Eurostar.

During that time in my life, money didn't matter. My business didn't matter. Nothing else mattered except this exhilarating feeling I had never felt before. For many months, I was consumed with feelings of euphoria, anxiety and excitement all at once.

I now understand why there is so much art and music dedicated to love. It is really mystical, euphoric, hypnotic and wonderful. Joining the club that I had always been left out of (the relationship club) felt really cool and special. As a proud member, I was ready to enjoy all the oxytocin that was flying around in my cells.

But long distance came with its challenges: both financial and practical. Looking back, I can see that I was definitely in a bit of a daze and not really connected to or aware of my money. Consideration for my finances didn't really enter the picture. I was still in a spending era, that's for sure, but I was not going to deny myself this expansive opportunity.

The cracks began to show in April 2025, and what followed were months of doubts, confusion and questioning. By July, my heart had shattered into a million pieces as the relationship officially came to an end: short lived, but very intense.

I spent weeks crying, unable to get out of bed, questioning the meaning of life, wearing only my pink fluffy dressing gown and living on a diet of cornflakes and ravioli. I had never experienced a pain like it. I could only liken it to grief – to grieve a person who is alive but not in my story anymore. The thought of showing up online was incomprehensible; I was barely able to show up for myself.

Everybody says your first heartbreak is the most painful, but no one can actually prepare for it. . . WOW. I felt like my heart was being ripped out of my chest. Excitement hadn't rushed through my veins in what felt like months. I nearly resigned myself to a life of sorrow and sadness. And as you can imagine, I certainly was not thinking about my money. . . I was in survival mode: the 'Looking after myself' era.

It is one thing to have your first heartbreak in your early twenties, when you maybe still live at home, with a part-time job you don't care about and university lectures you can afford to skip. It is another to be in your thirties and completely dependent on yourself.

During this time, I drew down all the remaining money I had saved. I had no choice. I was a single woman living in London, who ran her own business, with no rich family to fall back on and now, of course, no partner. I had only me, myself and I to rely on. It is what I was used to all my life, but it felt heavier this time round.

For multiple months (and what feels like nearly half of my 2025), I did what I needed to do at work to get by. I leaned on the money I had accumulated. I focused on mending my broken heart. This turned out to be the most transformative and eye-opening experience of my life. It was not my favourite financial era, but it was my most important.

AN ERA OF GROWTH AND DEVELOPMENT

The amount of growth I experienced as a human after the end of my relationship is impossible to put into words. I am NOT the same Laura I was back in September 2024 before I got hit round the head with the love stick. I am a different person, and my relationship with money is completely different too. I just had not realised yet. . .

And that voice note session with my coach Jessie that I described in Chapter 8 had reminded me of this fact: I teach people about the ebb and flow of money, and this time is no different for me.

During one of the most emotionally challenging times of my life (heartbreak), I was able to give myself the gift of time and space: the opportunity to truly feel my feelings and grieve, a priceless gift that I will cherish for the rest of my life.

It felt wonderful to acknowledge that I had been in a financial dip because I was using my money to support myself. Not many people have this: They either deny themselves of this or they actually don't have a choice. It is not realistic to quit your job, so you find yourself crying on lunchtimes in the office toilets. Some people have children, pets and responsibilities that they cannot ignore or isolate themselves from. How lucky that I had created a financial blanket that allowed me to snuggle under.

I was grateful that I gave myself that runway to feel the feels and cry it all out.

During those months when I grieved my relationship, I uncovered beliefs about myself and my life that I never even knew existed around love, self-worth, setting boundaries and the experience of being a human with emotions. Like an onion, peeling back layers and shedding so many things that no longer served me, I built back up a version of myself who was resilient yet open.

I did not return to the world with a closed-off heart or a bitterness for love. And on top of this, I also invested heavily in mindfulness retreats, 1:1 coaching and transformative experiences.

On paper, it looks like a step back financially.

But in my life, it felt like the biggest step forward.

After years of reading self-help books, digesting as much information online as I could about how to be more productive whilst not wasting time, top ways to be happy, lessons to live a fulfilled life (you get the picture!), I was never fully satisfied. There was a hum of urgency underneath my daily existence.

I was forever searching for new ways to feel contentment and peace, yet nothing seemed to stick. Then I was introduced to the world of the Three Principles framework by Sydney Banks and began coaching with Jessie.

It would be impossible to count the number of insights I had that set me free as I dived head-first into this new exciting world and 1:1 coaching (it was especially helpful whilst I battled heartbreak): I learnt how to be selfish in a good way and to put myself first; I strengthened my connection to my gut; I stopped crowdsourcing and always looking to other people for answers I already had inside of me; I understood the importance of my own needs and not being afraid to speak up for myself; I learnt where my creativity flourished and where my best work came from; I no longer feared commitment or intimacy; I felt true connection to my inner world and a sense of peace I'd never experienced before – my entire perspective on life shifted.

My relationship to my thoughts changed so dramatically that life looked and felt completely different. And I can never look back (good thing I don't want to!).

And during this time when insight after insight seemed to drop in, my relationship with money completely shifted too.

I might now be further away from financial independence and need to build up my savings and investments again, but I would spend every penny all over again to feel this level of freedom around my finances.

That is when I realised that my knowledge doesn't disappear, nor does my credibility, simply because I'm in a low season. In fact, learning how to share from the wound, not the scar, can be really powerful – I did not need to remain quiet on social media or hide away from my community. I was shaming myself so much that I completely forgot this.

I am who I am today because I accepted my financial era and allowed life to flow through me.

And to be clear, I am certainly not saying that this was my desired financial situation. But sometimes life happens to us, and the only thing we get to choose is how we react to that situation. You can have a financial goal and desire more money, while still being able to accept, appreciate and understand a change in your financial position along the journey.

Lean into your financial era and let go of: how you build wealth, financial consistency, or how your situation looks to others – and you will be the wealthiest person you know (regardless of the number in your bank account).

Chapter 10

Honouring Each Financial Era

When I look back, every financial era I've lived through has given me something different:

Each saving and investing era taught me discipline, consistency and to trust in my own abilities to hold on to my own money and build wealth. And it gave me the financial platform I needed to experience other seasons of my life.

My heartbreak 'survival' era showed me that money can be a form of safety, a cushion that holds you when your heart and mind need time to rest. *And boy oh boy, did I need solitude for a while.*

My fun spending eras (when I travelled and moved to London) revealed to me how life experiences can and will shape your identity, expand your world and deepen your courage.

My entrepreneurial era pushed me to use money in service of a dream, long before the outcome was guaranteed, creating opportunities for me that I could never have imagined.

Every financial era has a reason, a lesson or a learning.

I want to share five powerful reframes that can help you feel grounded throughout the transition of your financial eras, even if your current reality isn't what you'd hoped it would be. These will help you navigate financial seasons with grace, presence and personal power even when it feels like you're 'going backwards'.

KNOWLEDGE IS PERMANENT AND THAT MAKES YOU POWERFUL

Money can and will come and go. Circumstances change, but once you've built up financial knowledge and any other skills along the journey, they cannot be taken away from you. It is yours to keep and use – forever. It remains yours even during times when your net worth drops, you overspend, you dip into savings and investments and undo your 'financial progress'.

If you've learned how to budget, save, invest or build income before, and you've put it into practice, then you can do it again.

You're not starting from scratch; you already have knowledge and real experience.

Think of it like riding a bike: You might wobble or hit a bump and you might even fall off, but the skill doesn't disappear just because you're out of practice. Let this reminder restore your confidence: *You know what you're doing. You've done it before, so you'll do it again.*

But know that knowledge is information and wisdom is understanding. You get knowledge from learning, but you get wisdom from living. And the combination of the two will create a beautiful foundation for a fulfilled experience.

I saw a quote that said: '*The real measure of your financial wealth is how much you would be worth if you lost all your money*'. I love this sentiment.

Your mindset is the foundation of your financial success. Embracing the idea that all of your true financial wealth lies in your skills, knowledge, resilience and outlook shifts you from material wealth to personal empowerment. Your mindset will attract financial success to you and help you weather any financial storms with confidence. **You become unstoppable when you work on things that no one can take away from you – character, mindset and personality.**

YOUR CURRENT SITUATION IS NOT YOUR FINAL DESTINATION

Just because your investments are lower now, or your savings have taken a hit, or you're not making as much as you'd like in your business, it doesn't mean that's the end of your financial story. I promise you.

We see it threaded throughout stories of successful entrepreneurs, wealthy individuals and well-known celebrities.

When is a present moment ever a full indicator of your future? Rarely ever!

Think about the times you start a new job and you worry you'll never pick up all the systems and lingo, yet only six months later, everything feels completely second nature. Or think about when you decide to get fit and start working out. At first, the weights feel heavy, and your form feels awkward. You literally feel like you are never going to see progress. And then, slowly, the very things that once felt impossible become warm-up sets. You are no longer moaning and dragging yourself to the gym, but you are skipping along ready to move your limbs!

One of the most empowering shifts I believe you can make is to stop treating your *present* as a prophecy.

Life is dynamic, and things can change at any given moment, so what matters is what you do with what you have now, not what you think you 'should' have done earlier.

Each moment is an opportunity to try something new, think new thoughts and act differently.

Every future you want is built from small, grounded steps you take in the now.

MONEY IS MEANT TO BE USED, NOT JUST HOARDED

Yes, long-term investing is powerful, but so is using money to support your healing, health, growth and safety right now.

Maybe that looks like signing up for new therapy or coaching sessions, and it's an expense that eats into what you might be usually saving. Mental health is important, and it deserves a place in our budget sometimes. It is not frivolous or a waste of money.

It could be time off work to really rest to avoid burn-out or to grieve instead of burying feelings that will weigh you down later. Seriously, I heard someone say once '*Emotions buried alive resurrect*' years ago, and it stuck with me. It's best to feel them, let them rise and fall, because the body really does keep the score.

Or perhaps it's nourishing food to fuel your body, a well-needed holiday that helps reset your nervous system and bring you back home to yourself. If you are not feeling good and present within yourself, the wealth you are chasing will sooner rather than later make you feel completely empty inside. It is like a Lindt chocolate bunny that looks expensive from the outside, dripping in gold, but absolutely hollow and lifeless inside.

These are *not* irresponsible uses of money. They are evidence of your financial maturity and of learning that wealth isn't just about numbers, but it's also about supporting the whole of you and your life. The best gift you can give yourself is a life that feels supported, stable and aligned.

Money cannot offer any of these things if it just sits in a bank account without a purpose.

YOUR PEACE COMES FROM WITHIN, NOT FROM YOUR BANK BALANCE

The less meaning you assign to your bank balance as a measure of your worth, the more peace you'll feel. When your mind is clear, not crowded with judgement, you are present in your life and you become readily *available* to new ideas, new opportunities, creative solutions and grounded action.

If you're always telling yourself '*I've failed*' or '*My situation will never change*', your nervous system is on high alert, causing you to miss the quiet invitations of life. But when you feel safe within yourself, even if the external situation is messy, it becomes easier to spot the best next step to take in any situation – even if it doesn't always make sense to you in the moment.

Life can help show you the way, but you have to be willing to let it lead – trusting that you will always be okay no matter what, because peace is created first inside and then it reflects in your external world.

TWO THINGS CAN BE TRUE AT THE SAME TIME

It is possible to both desire more money and still be content with where you are. You can be grateful for what you have right now and still reach for what you want. These truths can coexist.

It is not an either–or situation. Wanting more money does not mean you are ungrateful, just as being grateful does not mean you will lose all your drive.

In fact, accepting the financial era you're currently in is what creates the mental and emotional room for your financial growth. When you stop fighting your reality, you free up energy to imagine something bigger for yourself because you are not caught up in worries about your present moment.

There is space to dream. Creativity awakens when shame and judgement are ignored. Possibilities you were once blind to now stare you in the face, making the correct next move seem obvious.

Meeting yourself with honesty and compassion in *this* era makes you far more available to receive the vision, insight and momentum that will carry you into your next one. This journey isn't linear, and how exciting it is!

BEING IN THE FLOW

Allow yourself to flow through your financial eras, not as an excuse for poor behaviour but as an understanding that your money ebbs and flows, much like life.

Have you ever done white water rafting? Your journey with money is a lot like that. You have *some* control like you can steer the raft, choose your line and adjust your approach, but life is the river you're flowing along.

When the water is calm, steering comes more easily. You can make deliberate moves, position yourself well and build momentum in the direction you want to go. But then you hit the rapids, and suddenly the water is tossing you around. In those moments, the best thing you can do is surrender to what you can't control. Do what you know how to do – protect yourself, stay safe and keep your paddle in the water. Getting through to the other side is what matters, and finding moments of joy along the way is part of it – even in the midst of pure chaos to varying degrees.

You might get soaking wet. You might be stuck in a rough rapid for longer than you hoped. And when you look around at the other rafters, you'll see all kinds of experiences: Some are drenched, battered and bruised, grinning ear to ear. Others made it through with barely a splash, their run somehow cleaner, calmer. Everyone's ride is different.

Life will always be doing its thing and you are the white water rafter. . . navigating your money in the best way you can, with the tools and skills you have. It is not meant to be a plain-sailing journey.

You can't control the river, but you can enjoy the ride. The more you lean in, let go of what you can't change and trust yourself in the raft, the better your chances of coming out the other side alive.

Now you know my full life story and how I have navigated my own financial eras and how freeing it is. I want to walk you through the 'how' with my ALIGN method.

PART III

Seeking Alignment

Chapter 11

The ALIGN Method

> 'Let your alignment (with Well-Being) be first and foremost, and let everything else be secondary, and not only will you have an eternally joyous journey, but everything you have ever imagined will flow effortlessly into your experience'.
>
> —*Esther Hicks/Abraham*

What are we truly seeking when we want to improve our relationship with money?

We are seeking **alignment**.

FROM MISALIGNMENT TO HARMONY

Alignment is the quiet but profound feeling of knowing your external actions are in harmony with your internal world. It is the end of an ongoing inner debate between who you are and what you do.

Often described as the experience of flow, acting from a place of alignment means there is minimal internal conflict or resistance because your energy is directed towards what truly matters to you moment to moment. Any friction, stress, overwhelm or noise in your life dramatically decreases, and your energy flows freely towards your goals and desires with the support from your inner wisdom.

Alignment lets your conscious desires become the driving force behind your actions. It bridges the gap between wanting and becoming. And when the part of you who wants wealth and your daily actions are in sync, creating wealth feels natural, abundance appears everywhere and your financial journey flows regardless of which era you're navigating.

Misalignment, on the other hand, feels heavy, slow and like you are attempting to swim through an ocean of treacle. It's the exhaustion of wanting one thing while confusingly doing another. It shows up in the guilt after each purchase you make because you told yourself you want to grow your savings, but you cannot stop spending.

Misalignment is when you know you deeply desire building wealth to have the freedom to travel the world or start a family, yet you avoid your bank account and listen to the fear that stops you from investing. It's the shame spirals that come from 'knowing better' but not doing better. It's living in perpetual contradiction, and I think we can all firmly say: Misalignment is draining.

You could break down alignment as the state where three core components of your life are working in perfect harmony, like the strings of a well-tuned instrument:

1. **Your Thinking:** These are the thoughts you have and the meaning you make of money, in relation to yourself and the world (e.g. 'I am capable of success' or 'Money is hard to earn' or 'People like me never make a lot of money').
2. **Your Values:** These are the non-negotiable guiding principles in your life (e.g. freedom, honesty, connection, generosity and adventure) that define your true north in life.
3. **Your Actions:** This is simply what you do and how you behave every day (e.g. how you spend, how you save and how you communicate).

True, sustainable alignment happens when your actions are congruent with both your deeply held values and your thinking.

If your thinking supports scarcity, your actions will be inconsistent and frantic, creating financial dissonance along your financial journey. When all three are consistent, everything flows, your life is clear and you move with ease.

INTRODUCING THE ALIGN METHOD

In this part of the book, I am so excited to introduce you to the ALIGN method. It is a set of tools, practices, mindsets, habits and lifestyles you can implement to change your relationship with money. The next few chapters will help you create both instant relief and long-lasting financial ease and peace in your own life so money serves as a tool, not a trap.

Digesting this method and implementing ALIGN in your own way will help you break free from autopilot and stop searching for answers about your financial relationship outside of yourself. Finally, you will be able to consciously create useful and supportive money behaviours, allowing you to intentionally build wealth without stress.

The five steps of ALIGN are the following:

- **A – Awareness and Acceptance**
- **L – Living in the Now**
- **I – Imagine**
- **G – Guide Your Mind**
- **N – Navigate with Aligned Action**

The first two steps are the practice of observing without attachment – taking an unfiltered look at your relationship with yourself and money and then loosening your grip so you no longer identify with old stories and patterns, creating space for something new. **AWARENESS** will teach you how to look honestly at your money story, your current financial reality and the thought patterns that have been running your life on autopilot. And **ACCEPTANCE** will show you how to release any judgement, accept what is and what has been, and stop resisting the very reality you're trying to change. **LIVING IN THE NOW** will share the power of getting present, learning how to experience life in the moment without constantly dragging yourself back into the experience of the past. These two steps pose the questions: *Who am I when I stop believing my thoughts? Who am I when I stop automatically believing everything my mind says about money?*

Once space has been created, the next two steps are about intentional creation and mental reconditioning. You are envisioning a new future and then training your mind to sustain it. You are consciously harnessing the power of your mind to reshape your inner world and create a new identity. **IMAGINE** will open up possibilities, helping you explore what wealth actually means to you and who you're becoming as you create it. **GUIDE YOUR MIND** will give you the tools to retrain your thoughts to match your new identity, shift your internal dialogue and build new beliefs that stick. These two steps pose the questions: *What can I create if I train my mind in a new direction? Who can I become when I drive my mind, not the other way round*?

And the final step finishes off with integrating it all into your daily life, turning actions into habits and ensuring inner work becomes outer results. You'll make different decisions from your new internal state and take action that aligns with your values and goals, creating your new financial reality. **NAVIGATE WITH ALIGNED ACTION** will ground everything in real, aligned action so you can live life as a new you and create tangible results with your finances. This final step asks the questions: *How can I integrate this work to become fully aligned? How do I move through the world as this new version of myself?*

Together, these five steps create a complete transformation – one that honours both the wisdom of surrender and the power of creation.

The ALIGN method is designed to guide you back home to yourself. It teaches you how to work *with* your mind rather than against it, and how to show up in your financial life in a way that actually moves you forward.

This is about learning how to change your relationship with money and to build wealth without the constant distractions, self-sabotage or confusion that may be holding you back right now. You can say bye to 'being better' with money through sheer willpower and uncover what is *true* for you because when your financial decisions begin to flow from your truth, ease replaces effort, your progress becomes sustainable and I know it sounds kind of crazy. . . but your financial journey becomes enjoyable.

If at any point you notice resistance, avoidance or discomfort as you read, let that be information rather than evidence of failure because alignment starts with honesty.

Chapter 12

A – Awareness and Acceptance

Let's dive into the first step of the ALIGN method, starting with awareness and acceptance.

> 'Not everything that is faced can be changed, but nothing can be changed until it is faced'.
>
> —*James Baldwin*

Awareness is the first step on the staircase. It is the non-negotiable starting point of all and any change, and I am going to hold your hand when I say this: You cannot avoid it.

Trying to change your relationship with money without any level of awareness is like trying to make a new meal without ever looking at the recipe. You just go in the cupboard, you grab what you can find, you shove it all in the pot and pray for the best. Sometimes that might work out, but 99% of the time, it is going to be an inedible mess and a waste of time.

You have to open your eyes first.

Awareness is not a YouTube ad you can pay a premium to skip, or a long traffic jam you can reroute on your SatNav. It is the golden gate you have to walk through. But once you get to the other side, you find yourself in a magical land where the soil is fertile for true change. It becomes the foundation for building the life you actually want to live.

WHY DO WE AVOID AWARENESS?

If awareness is a necessary step ultimately leading us to more freedom, peace and fulfilment (and of course alignment), then why do people avoid it? Why are people so scared to look inside, reflect on the past, notice their actions and be fully honest about how they are currently living?

I think society has a part to play in that! Somewhere down the line, we were taught that 'ignorance is bliss'. But this rings true only when you apply it to things you cannot, or should not, change.

But when it comes to your finances, avoidance does not protect you. There is a well-known phrase called 'ostriching' – the concept of sticking your head in the sand and ignoring all problems you have with money.

Avoiding your own truth (e.g. not paying attention to your bank balance or how you talk about money) reveals a fear or doubt in your ability to make change: the belief that if you just stay oblivious or ignorant, you can avoid the pain of changing (or avoid the pain that comes with thinking we *can't* change).

When it comes to awareness, the source of pain does not come from what you find. It is not the truth about your situation that causes the discomfort.

The suffering actually comes from the size of the gap between knowing something and taking action on it.

The bigger the gap, the more we suffer. And that gap is widened when we make meaning out of what we find. It acts as a barrier to taking action.

So many of us go through life scared to see what lies beneath, scared to know the truth and scared to know ourselves in case we discover something we don't like – or, even worse, in fear of finding something we *believe* is unchangeable.

But all this does is keep us stuck. . . and pretty darn miserable.

A lack of awareness eventually leads to an intensifying pain, and your life remains exactly the same.

Therefore, increasing your awareness is the ultimate power move, not something to fear because the intense temporary sting of honest self-awareness beats the slow ache of an unfulfilling life.

I listened to a beautiful podcast episode on *Inspired by Emma Grede* with Tracey Ellis Ross where she said: '***I am learning every day to allow the space between where I am and where I want to be to inspire me and not terrify me'.***

This is the shift awareness creates. Instead of the gap between your current reality and your desired future feeling like evidence of failure or a prediction about your future or an extension of who you are, it can instead simply be *information*. It becomes a map to move forward, and it will be impossible to close a gap you refuse to acknowledge exists.

Awareness demands that you look inward, but this is where your true financial exploration begins.

Root Awareness (Looking at Your Past/Your Childhood)

Root awareness is looking back into your past with interest and curiosity to identify the origins, experiences and unconscious situations that influence the thoughts you have about money today.

Root awareness asks:

- What role did money play throughout my childhood?
- What memories, emotions and experiences do I recall from my upbringing that shaped my perspective on money today?
- What did I learn about money from the adults around me?
- What words or phrases do I remember hearing growing up?
- How do I think society, culture or religion played a role in how I think about money?

This introspection can give you context, and it can help you understand the *why* behind your actions up until this point. You can draw lines and join dots between the way you think and feel now and the source of your behaviours.

But please know this is not an exercise that has to be done with intense rigour. You are not a detective trying to solve a murder.

We all have that one friend who should be part of the FBI, right? You mention to her that you saw a cute guy at the coffee shop but didn't get a chance to ask for his number and that all you have is this sneaky photo of him.

BOOM, before you know it, her deep search into the Internet is underway. She has found his social media, his home address, who he banks with and the medical history of his own mother.

You do not need to go searching into your own past with the same level of intensity as your secret agent friend.

Instead, take a more gentle approach. . . '*hmmm, let's get a little bit curious here, I wonder what has influenced me today, maybe I will find something useful, and maybe I won't*'.

From this light-hearted attitude, you can uncover potentially interesting information about your past that might help you understand yourself better.

You Cannot Unring the Bell

Sometimes one moment of true awareness can be worth years of therapy, courses or self-help books because **you can't unring the bell.**

Whether it is looking back at the past or realising your thinking in the present moment, once you have 'seen' something differently or learned something new that changes your perspective, you can never go back to before. How beautiful to be having this experience where we have awareness of ourselves – a consciousness – that allows us to have more control over our lives.

One time, after hosting a Money Mindset workshop, a woman approached me with tears in her eyes and said (and I paraphrase. . .) '*Laura, I have to tell you, I just had the most beautiful insight. I realised that I have been a huge spender my whole life, and to be honest, I never understood why. But what you have shared today has reminded me of something that I had forgotten or maybe blocked out. My mum used to take us on huge shopping sprees when I was younger to get out of the house, away from my dad. He never cared what we bought. . . He never cared about anything. I realise now that for my mum it was probably a cry for help or a bid for attention. But the funny thing is, I don't even like shopping! I have convinced myself for years that it is what I love to do and it is just part of my personality and who I am. But actually, if I am honest, I don't think it IS who I am. I have been so influenced by my mum's behaviour. I feel like a weight has been lifted!*'

How beautiful. What a life-changing moment of awareness this is.

She didn't need to spend months in therapy dissecting her childhood and rehashing her entire past.

She just needed one clear moment of seeing the connection between then and now, and suddenly, the pattern that had controlled her for decades lost its grip. Does it mean she will never shop again? No. But the simple moment of awareness puts space between how she has been behaving and how she will behave moving forward. It showed her she had a choice.

Once you see it, you can't unsee it. The bell has been rung.

A Tool to Help: Journalling

One of my favourite tools for my own personal development is simple and cheap: journalling.

When I was 18, I read the infamous Julia Cameron book *The Artist's Way*.

A concept she asks you to use to begin your journey to self-discovery and creativity is called the Morning Pages. The aim is to fill up two A4 pages of writing (or drawing) every single morning before you start your day, an opportunity to get anything in your mind out onto paper and out of your head.

That book, amongst a few others such as *The Power of Now* and *There Is a Spiritual Solution to Every Problem*, sent me down a path of self-discovery. During some extremely challenging times in my life, my entry into the personal development world was perfectly timed, and this journalling practice created a blank page (no pun intended) for me to discover my inner workings, deep desires and so much more.

It became a safe space to increase awareness of what was going on inside of me and admit to myself what I was not ready to share with other people.

The best part is that no one has to read your journal. It is private. So, the only person you would be lying to when answering these questions is yourself.

Visit https://www.findyourwealthbook.com/resources to get access to a list of my money journal prompts to help you explore your past and deepen your journalling practice.

Answering these questions can build up a useful picture of what's influenced your thoughts and feelings about money today because you can start to make connections and links to your reality now. It's not the whole picture, but it can be a great place to start.

The interesting thing is everything is connected: **Your past with money doesn't just shape your finances, but it can also shape your entire sense of self and how you show up in the world.**

Financial experiences from your past can distort your reality now in ways that bleed into every area of your life.

For instance, if growing up with little money meant you were bullied at school for wearing thrifted clothes (before thrifting was actually cool), you might now believe you're 'not creative' or 'not fashionable', simply because you never had the resources to express yourself.

Years later, you might yearn for a career in fashion but have convinced yourself it's not meant for you. The meaning you are making out of your past makes you doubt your own creative abilities. Conflict was created between who you are at your core (a creative being) and who you believe you are (what the kids at school said).

But your financial past does not need to block the exploration of this new creative career path.

Also, your troubled relationship with money won't always originate from financial hardship or trauma in your past.

Sometimes your relationship with money has nothing to do with money at all.

Maybe your financial childhood was perfectly fine – stable, comfortable and no obvious issues. But other things happened that shaped how you handle money now.

Maybe your parents split up when you were a teenager and you were devastated, and somewhere along the way you started using shopping to make yourself feel better. Maybe you were supposed to be an athlete, had your entire future mapped out, and then you broke your ankle and had to completely rethink who you were and all that grief, confusion and loss of identity got channelled into overspending or hoarding money or avoiding financial decisions altogether.

Your relationship with money might just be the by-product of an entirely different internal battle or struggle.

Your financial behaviour – the overspending, the debt, the avoidance, or anything that feels misaligned with your desires – is just the visible symptom of something else going on underneath. It's how your pain or confusion or sadness or fear showed up in your adult world.

So, when you're doing this root awareness work, exploring your past to understand your present patterns, don't limit yourself to only looking at financial events or money-related experiences. You should feel free to explore questions like: What was happening in your life when certain money patterns started? What were you feeling? What were you dealing with? What did you need that you weren't getting?

Sometimes the answer to 'Why am I like this with money?' has absolutely nothing to do with money itself. It's just one of the places where your inner world gets expressed because as we now know: **Behaviour is just an indicator of your inner world and how much you are making meaning out of your thinking moment to moment.**

It's all part of the tapestry of how we become who we are with money. And root awareness is a beautiful place to begin.

Present Awareness (Your Current Thinking, Actions and Reality)

Present awareness (or financial mindfulness) is the subtle moment-to-moment observation of your thoughts, feelings, habits and actions right now.

Present awareness asks:

- What is my current financial situation and how do I think and feel about it?
- What stories am I telling myself about money right now?
- What's happening in my body when I make financial decisions?
- What's going on inside me right before I spend/save/invest?

When you begin to notice what is going on in the moment, you can provide yourself with a different option – a new way of behaving. You realise you have more choice, and you do not have to repeat the same patterns as before.

If root awareness is the map showing you where you have been and how you got where you are today, present awareness is the compass that helps you move forward to where you want to go. The map is nice to have but not necessary. The compass is essential for reaching your destination.

Please don't assume that you have to stay 'on top of' yourself constantly. You do not have to be aware of every single thought you have or monitor every action moment to moment.

Hypervigilance can be just as tiring as avoidance or a lack of awareness. We're not here to try to notice everything constantly. In fact, it is quite the opposite.

When it comes to this present awareness, the aim is to cultivate more of a calm and peaceful awareness, noticing without any judgement.

As you practise present awareness, you're simply gathering information:

- When do I feel anxious about money?
- What triggers my urge to spend?
- What thoughts show up when I check my bank account?
- How does my body feel when I make financial decisions?

You're not trying to fix anything yet. You're not trying to stop the thoughts or change the behaviours. You're just seeing them clearly because the very act of noticing often begins the process of change, without you having to force anything.

ACCEPTANCE: THE BRIDGE BETWEEN SEEING AND CHANGING

> 'The first step toward change is awareness. The second step is acceptance'.
>
> —*Nathaniel Branden*

Awareness and acceptance together are a powerful potion for change, and the ingredients live inside of you. If you can take an honest look at your life without any attachment to what you find, you create the perfect foundation for transformation.

Once you have begun the process of awareness, your question might be: '*What do I do with all this new information I have gathered about myself?*'

And do you know what, that is a great question!

Many people become aware of their thoughts and behaviours but immediately declare war on themselves. Judgement and shame walk into the party without an invitation and try to force change through willpower and brutal self-criticism, using punishment as a catalyst for better financial behaviour.

Self-loathing as a strategy for personal growth does not work.

That's right, hating on yourself, shaming yourself and being annoyed at yourself is not a good way to change your life and maintain any useful or healthy financial habits.

Judgement may have turned up to the party without an invite, but it does not have to be the DJ controlling the music or curating the vibe. You can let it sit in the corner quietly, giving it no attention.

Noticing is awareness – nothing more, nothing less. It is simply observing what is. But judging is adding a layer of noise on top of what you observe.

For example:

- Noticing: 'I spent outside of my budget today'.
- Judging: 'I spent too much money today, and I am a failure and irresponsible with my money'.

or

- Noticing: 'I would like to have more money in my savings so I can buy a house'.
- Judging: 'Why am I so bad at saving?', 'Will I ever reach my own goal of buying a house?', 'I cannot believe I am so behind everyone else; what is the point in trying?'

The first is a neutral observation. The second is a story you're telling yourself about what that observation means about you as a person, your life or your future.

A Spiritual Being Having a Human Experience

When you notice a thought, pause and ask yourself a simple but profound question: '*Who is noticing that thought? If I was the thought, then who is the one aware of it right now?*'

You are simply the observer watching thoughts go by like clouds passing across the sky.

That observer is not the thought itself, but rather the consciousness that's aware of the thought.

Thoughts aren't facts about who you are; they're just 'mental weather' passing through your inner landscape.

You are a spiritual being having a human experience, which includes the experience of thought. Understanding this makes acceptance a natural part of the process instead of a step you must master.

Most of us move through life mistaking thoughts as identity.

The thought '*I'm bad with money*' doesn't feel like just a thought; it feels like an undeniable fact about who you are as a person.

The thought '*I'll never get ahead*' doesn't feel like one interpretation amongst many possibilities; it feels like your inevitable destiny, already carved in stone.

The thought '*I always mess this up*' doesn't feel like a story your mind is telling; it feels like your core identity, the unchangeable truth of who you've always been and who you'll always be.

Realising you're the observer lets you experience thought without believing it's an eternal truth about your character or capabilities. Understanding the temporary nature of thought – always moving through us, changing like weather – helps you release attachment to your thinking.

Sometimes your thinking is so fast or habitual you might not realise that it is creating the discomfort in your body. Regardless of how long a thought pattern has existed, at any moment you can swap identifying *with* the thought, to simply observing it. Letting thoughts be there and trusting they can and will move through you is powerful.

Emotions are the same – simply an experience in your body. Feelings, like thoughts, come and go throughout your day.

You can notice anxiety rippling through your body when you check your bank balance without deciding that this anxiety means something is fundamentally wrong with you as a person.

You can notice the overwhelm you feel when you think about the cash flow in your business without making meaning out of it and deciding your future is doomed and the business should shut down.

You can see the pattern of overspending clearly, study it with genuine curiosity and gather useful information about what triggers it – all without believing that you're broken or defective or somehow incapable of change.

Because you're not any of those things. You're the awareness observing all of it, and that awareness is always whole, always okay, always capable of making a different choice in the next moment.

Think about a time when you were in a really bad mood. . . something upset you or annoyed you, and before you know it, you were feeling agitated, angry and overwhelmed. At some point, that emotion moved through you. Maybe it was a few days later, maybe a few hours later in the day or maybe even a few minutes went by and you felt your mood shift.

However long or short, emotion always shifts.

Let me give you a specific example with money because this is where we often forget that emotions are temporary.

You check your bank account and see an unexpected charge, or get an email about a bill you forgot was due, or a client backs out of a deal they agreed to, leaving you short for the month. Immediately, anxiety floods your body. Your chest tightens, your stomach drops and your mind starts spiralling.

> 'How am I going to cover this? I'm never going to get ahead. I can't believe this is happening again'.

In that moment, the anxiety feels absolutely all-consuming and permanent, like it's going to swallow you whole. In that moment, it can be hard to imagine feeling calm or okay about your finances ever again. The emotion is so intense, so present, that it feels like your entire reality.

But then something happens.

Maybe a few hours later, a friend texts you something funny and you laugh, like genuinely laughing that kind of belly laugh that gives you abs (my favourite feeling in the world), and for those few seconds you completely forget you are anxious about money.

Maybe the next day, you wake up and the panic isn't quite as intense – it's still there but you can breathe a little easier. Maybe you have a conversation with someone, or you go for a walk, or you figure out a small solution to part of the problem, and suddenly the overwhelming anxiety has shifted into something more manageable.

It's like you're a completely different person having a completely different experience.

You do not need something external about your money to change for your emotions to shift.

Emotions shift regardless. Even when nothing changes externally, the intensity of the emotion moves through you – always every single time.

This is the nature of emotion.

But when you're in the middle of intense financial anxiety, consumed by fear or stress or panic about money, I know it can feel almost impossible to remember this truth. It feels like this is your permanent state, like you'll always feel this terrible about money and like the anxiety is who you are now rather than what you're experiencing right now.

And because it feels permanent, we do things to try to make it stop immediately.

Without the understanding of how emotion works, we very innocently attempt to shift our emotion to experience something different.

We avoid looking at our finances (trying to make the anxiety go away by not facing it).

We emotionally spend (trying to soothe the bad feeling with a purchase).

We eat comfort food, drink alcohol and smoke cigarettes (to get a quick hit of dopamine!).

And sometimes, we try to 'think our way into a new feeling'.

We think through every possible solution to this problem (as if our busy minds will have the answers we need readily available).

We spiral into worst-case scenarios (as if catastrophising will somehow prepare us or protect us).

We beat ourselves up (as if shame will prevent us from making the same mistake again).

But none of that is necessary. Because the emotion is already moving through us. It's already going to shift, change and eventually pass, whether you do anything about it or not.

What if you could remember, in the middle of the financial anxiety, that this feeling is temporary? What if you could feel the panic in your chest and know that it won't last forever, that it's already moving through you and at some point it will shift, because it always does.

Of course, you will still experience feelings of anxiety, but you wouldn't need to make it mean something permanent about you or your financial future. You could just let it be here, knowing it will pass in its own time.

Uncomfortable? Yes. Permanent? Absolutely not.

To be human is to feel.

How wonderful to experience life to its fullest with a wide range of emotions ranging from love, joy, contentment, awe and excitement through to intense sadness, loss, grief, confusion and pain.

And if you want to experience all of the 'good' emotions intensely, know that the pendulum has to swing both ways and you will also experience the 'bad' emotions intensely too. And you will always be okay.

If you have ever gone through any type of heartbreak, you will know that you never stay in one emotion forever.

2025 was the first time I experienced extremely low feelings for months in a row. As a generally optimistic and positive person, in times of hardship I usually can still find and feel joy. But this time round it was different: I would wake up every day, open my eyes and be like 'wow I don't think I will ever feel happy again'. All the things that used to bring me joy felt pointless and empty. It felt like sadness lived in every cell of my body.

Then one day. . . I felt different.

A little bit of joy re-entered my orbit, things started making me laugh, and I got to experience awe and wonder again. What I have learnt from my pain is that pain (and any other perceived negative emotion) is only temporary.

If the point of being human is to feel and to experience and to enjoy – how exciting to go into every new experience with open arms, enjoying it moment to moment as it shifts and changes.

Accepting Your Financial Starting Point

I wasn't raised in a wealthy family. I grew up in a working-class household with two brothers, a sister and two parents who worked full-time just to keep us afloat. Hand-me-downs were the norm. Eating out was a special occasion, not something we casually did on a Tuesday.

As the eldest daughter, there were responsibilities and burdens that came along with my place in a big family without much money, and I felt like I became an adult from a very early age. I was hyper-aware of financial concerns and struggles my parents faced. I saved my own money only to have to lend it out often, and I never asked for anything expensive at Christmas or on birthdays.

Accepting my financial starting point meant facing a simple truth: Some people started way ahead of me. They had access to resources, education and safety nets I never had. Their race began on a completely different track.

Some people are further ahead than you right now, even if you started at the same time. Some are behind you, dealing with challenges you can't even imagine. Life hands out the cards before we even sit at the table, and no one gets to swap hands at the start.

You can spend your life furious about the cards you were dealt. . . or you can decide how you're going to play them.

There are many 'rags-to-riches' stories: Someone born into dire circumstances defeats all odds stacked against them to create a very wealthy life. These always give me hope.

As Linda Pransky said on the *What Moves You with Jessie* podcast: '*Hope is the bridge to a new feeling. And anything is possible with hope*'.

But hope cannot exist without acceptance.

If you're constantly resisting where you are – replaying what you didn't have, resenting what others have and fighting your starting point like it personally did you dirty – there's no room for hope. You're too busy being at war with reality to imagine a different future.

Acceptance doesn't mean *liking* where you are. It just means seeing it clearly for what it is.

Acceptance creates the soil where hope can grow, the foundation that lets you build a different future.

You never really know someone's financial background just by looking at them or seeing what they post on social media. You don't know if they were born into a financially comfortable family or how much they've struggled behind closed doors. You can't see how they're actually feeling inside about money, the anxiety they might wake up with in the middle of the night or what's actually in their bank account vs. what they're projecting to the world.

So when you stop resisting and choose to accept your own financial starting point, you can decide what you're going to do next. **Your past does not need to be your future, and your starting point doesn't determine your destination.**

Non-acceptance can show up in the form of resentment.

Carrie Fisher said it best: '*Resentment is like drinking poison and waiting for the other person to die*'.

If you resent your parents for not teaching you about money, that resentment isn't hurting them – it is only hurting you. Resenting them does not automatically install a financial education into your brain.

If you resent an ex-partner for the financial mess they left behind – the debt, the stress, the clean-up – you're still dragging the emotional equivalent of a suitcase with a broken wheel. That's heavy stuff! Resenting them does not automatically pay off your debt and improve your credit score.

If you resent a friend or colleague who seems to 'have it all figured out', that resentment doesn't reduce their success. Resenting them does not automatically speed up your success.

Resentment just robs you of peace and keeps you focused on the very opposite feeling you would like to experience. Letting go of resentment is choosing to put the poison down.

> 'If you wanna fly, you got to give up the shit that weighs you down'.
>
> —*Toni Morrison*

Awareness is what shows you the patterns clearly, helps you see what's been happening with your money, where these patterns originated in your past and how they're playing out in your life right now in concrete ways.

Observation is what reminds you that you're not actually those patterns themselves, that you're the consciousness watching them unfold and the awareness that can step back and see what's happening without being completely consumed by it or identified with it.

And acceptance is what allows you to stop fighting the patterns, to release the exhausting battle you've been waging against yourself and to finally put down the weapons and make peace with what is, so you can work with it instead of against it.

Imagine a world where you choose not to believe every thought that crosses your mind – where you see them for what they are – stories and books you're reading. Imagine how much lighter and clearer you would feel. How much more time you would have to create and make money and enjoy your days. How much better you'd sleep and how much more energy you'd have. It sounds pretty dreamy, right?

The magic lies in not taking any financial situation and adding layers of noise to it.

Chapter 13

L – Living in the Now

Now that you can see the value in becoming aware and having true acceptance, we can explore what it means to be truly present and live in the now.

All we have *is* the now. When this concept lands, it hits home in the most profound way and you cannot unsee it (even if you forget it). There is no past or future – they both only exist in the now, happening through our conscious thinking. The past only exists in our memories. The future only exists in our plans and dreams. The present is our only reality. Life is literally just a series of moments happening right now and that is where all the magic and our true power lie.

> 'This very moment is the perfect teacher, and, lucky for us, it's with us wherever we are'.
>
> —*Pema Chodron*

Reading *The Power of Now* by Eckhart Tolle gave me an existential crisis followed by a blissful epiphany, as it created the portal to my own contentment in any given moment. Freeing yourself from the prison of thought and learning to live in the now is the path to everything you desire. True wealth resides in the present. I continue to learn this daily on a deeper but simpler level.

When you live moment to moment, you let go of the past and create space for the future, increasing your connection to your wisdom. It enhances the senses that allow you to perceive the world, resulting in aligned decisions and a more colourful existence – the most magical way to live, experiencing it as it happens.

This doesn't mean you can't reminisce about beautiful memories or plan ahead. It means not being consumed by what was or what could be.

And the more you practise presence, the more at ease you feel with money. You build wealth without attachment. Your financial life unfolds naturally, keeping you open to opportunities beyond what your mind could imagine. This is how you create a healthy, stress-free relationship with money.

Living in the now sounds pretty awesome, right? It is the answer to a lot of your 'problems'.

THE WHISPERS OF YOUR SOUL ARE LOUDER WHEN YOU ARE PRESENT

When you have a problem in your life, how do you go about solving it?

Do you confide in your close ones to source opinions? Do you pray to something bigger than you for clarity? Do you create a mind map of thoughts or list out the pros and cons?

Maybe you go for a walk or take a nap or a shower.

It could be a combination, and maybe it changes depending on the situation you find yourself in.

But the key question here is: *How do you know when your intuition is telling you something?*

Every person and situation is different. But at some point, you get clarity.

A solution, an idea or a next step to take reveals itself to you in some way. And the answer is always '*I don't know how I knew, I just did*' or '*the idea just popped out of nowhere!*'.

You may not always realise it, believe it or follow it, but the wisdom is always there inside of you. And it is waiting for you to get quieter inside so it can reveal itself to you.

Sometimes, an opportunity presents itself to you almost randomly, making the situation you're in feel lighter. Or an idea comes out of nowhere and helps you see the way through it or at least one good next step ahead. Or a strong feeling in your body that you just can't explain but reveals the answer to your question.

This knowing inside of you allows you to take a step back from stressing over your financial situation, and you let the answer reveal itself to you instead of searching for it in your mind.

When you're present with life following the nudges moment to moment – not caught up in your thoughts about your finances – everything will unfold as it needs to. You will always be taken care of.

You won't accidentally end up just spending all your money, driving your finances into the ground and being poor and broke and on the streets.

Instead, being tapped into the very flow of life itself and open to the opportunities around you is where the magic happens.

Your intuition, gut, wisdom – whatever you like to call it – will always guide you.

FROM CROWDSOURCING TO TRUSTING MYSELF

From a very young age, I accidentally learned to ignore my own intuition because listening to myself felt unsafe. For most of my life, I used to say: '*I don't have a "gut feeling". It has never existed in me*'.

Throughout my school years, I had a rough time. I was in the 'popular group', but I was also the scapegoat. Each day, it felt like my 'best friends' decided whether they liked me or not.

I share this not so you pity me. I don't need a pity party. And let's be real here; I imagine that most people had challenging school years in one way or another. And I genuinely do not harbour any hate, anger or resentment towards those girls. Looking back on my school years, I have compassion for them. I can see that they all had their own troubles and challenges, but unfortunately, I often became their punching bag as a way of them coping with their own shit.

Over time, I learnt to survive by blending in with their decisions. It was safer for me to be super easygoing with plans and keeping my opinions quiet so that I wouldn't accidentally say the wrong thing, leaving me open to scrutiny. I moulded myself to fit whatever the group needed. So by the time I was an adult, I felt like I had no clue how to make decisions for myself.

Many decisions throughout my twenties were influenced by something called 'crowdsourcing'.

I would speak to everyone about my problems and concerns. I'd strategically, sometimes frantically, gather information from friends, family, the Internet and strangers in comment sections. Then, I'd pick the most common answer or the strongest one, which more often than not meant ignoring my own wants or needs.

I genuinely believed I didn't 'have a gut'. But my gut wasn't missing; it was just buried underneath years of worry and noise. It was crushed underneath the weight of my thinking.

There's a phrase I love: '*Worry looks around. Trust looks within*'.

I was so busy looking around – seeking validation, approval and consensus – that I couldn't hear the quiet voice inside myself.

It wasn't until I reached my thirties that I truly learnt how to trust my own judgement. I realised that there are no right or wrong decisions. There are only decisions: You make them right, or you figure out your next move after that.

Think about it: How many times have you agonised over making the 'wrong' decision in your life, only to have it turn out fine?

I used to stress the hell out of deciding everything and anything – from decisions as small as what to order at the restaurant for dinner or which seat to choose on the plane up to the big decisions such as whether to go to university and when to quit my job. Yet, after every decision I have ever made, I have always been okay.

Perfection does not exist. If you focus less on making the 'right choice' and more on working with the choice you make, life will get a whole lot more enjoyable. Because in the end, after every decision you have ever made, you were always okay.

I am sure you can think of a time when you made a decision and the worst-case scenario occurred. The thing you didn't want to happen, happened. You think '*ugh I should have chosen the other option*'.

Maybe you made an investment choice that cost you thousands of pounds. Maybe you chose to lend money to a friend, and you never saw it back again. Maybe you quit your job to go to a new one, but it didn't work out how you thought it would. . . No matter what happened, you were and are still okay.

The more pressure you put on every decision you make, the harder it is to make decisions.

Over time, the more you understand that you will always be okay with any decision you make, the more relaxed you become. And the more relaxed you are, the more connected you become to your own inner guidance system. That quiet voice is always giving you little hints and clues about where to go next and what move to make.

The wisdom that lives inside of you is a sense of calm and peace that you have a connection to. It guides you through life in every decision you make. Sometimes you are aware of it and sometimes you are not.

But you must know that this wisdom is not in your thoughts.

Underneath all the noise of thought is your connection to something deeper.

Every single one of us, including you, reading this book right now, has a deep wisdom inside greater than our thinking – a wisdom that will forever be our guiding light throughout life.

This is the wisdom that knows when to save and when to spend, that allows the flow of your financial life, regardless of which season you're in, that helps you identify the next aligned step to take and that comes up with random ideas that seem disconnected from the problem at hand yet lead you to something that changes everything.

Making decisions about you, your money and your life becomes easier when you realise that this wisdom already lives inside of you. It always has and it always will, even when it gets buried under the weight of thinking.

LETTING GO AND TAPPING IN

Let me tell you a story about the beautiful time when I learnt for myself the power of letting go.

At the start of January 2025, I was really struggling in my business. I came into the new year with no prospects, a quiet inbox and an empty pipeline of potential opportunities. I was freaking out, going into 'overdrive', and spent each day sitting and staring at my laptop and constantly going to the fridge to look for snacks to get some light relief from my frustrating procrastination.

I was so scared that if I stopped worrying about my financial situation, then I would end up in a worse position. I feared that the days would fly by, I would run my business into the ground and I would go bankrupt.

But there is a big difference between being mindful and stressing yourself out stuck in loops of thoughts that keep you in an ungrounded state.

I was scared that being present, enjoying my life moment to moment, following the nudges of where my energy was begging me to go or taking part in any activities unrelated to money was pointless, irresponsible and not the solution. I used to worry that if my financial problems were not constantly on my mind, then the problems would get worse.

Wow, I couldn't have been more wrong.

Constantly thinking about my problems kept all my energy and attention focused in the wrong direction. I was living inside of my head and missing out on the very opportunities to shift my energy, create more money and find solutions.

After some wonderful calls with my coach Jessie, I realised that I was so overwhelmed with fear and stress that all I was doing was making my situation so much worse. I couldn't think straight.

Everything felt overwhelming.

And ironically, doing anything in the business, which is how I would call in the money, felt scary and near impossible. I was paralysed.

It was time to release the hold on my old way of thinking and lean into trust that anything can shift at any moment – what else did I have to lose?!

I welcomed a new perspective to see my situation differently and waited for the new ideas that could help. I did not go in search of them frantically; I trusted instead that when I got more present in life, the ideas would naturally find me.

What this looked like in practice was a combination of things; I chose to meditate more to help my mind to quieten and not react to my thoughts. I focused on physical movement like yoga or walks especially when I started to feel stagnant or blocked or angsty. I did things that got me into a flow state, creating a connection to the presence of life. I socialised with my favourite people and laughed nights away.

None of these actions are a blueprint to financial wealth, but simply what felt right for me to do at that moment in time. I listened to myself daily and then ideas about what to do next flowed in, which most of the time felt completely unrelated to making money. . . but I listened anyway.

This was not me ignoring my problems or avoiding the situation. I was instead creating room for something different, something new and something fresh!

Mind you, I really had no clue what the hell was going to happen. I went in blind.

It reminds me of that image of someone holding onto the edge of a cliff with one hand so scared to let go for fear of falling a great height. The universe is saying '*Let go first and trust I will catch you*', and as soon as they do, they realise that the ground was not far away from their feet at all – so beautiful.

A few weeks later, I was on my coaching call. I shared my panic. I had started looking on a job recruitment website for full-time jobs. I had a moment of fear. All I could think was '*Nothing is changing, clearly this isn't working*'.

I remember Jessie asking me '*Do you want to get a 9–5 job? Does that feel like what you want to do right now?*'

She reminded me that there is no right or wrong answer, it was not a leading question, but an opportunity for me to get quiet and be honest with myself about the energy behind what I was doing. And whether this idea came from my busy, fearful mind or from my inner wisdom. . .

Now, whilst I have absolutely no shame in going back into a 9–5 job if it felt the right thing to do. . . the answer came through loud and clear, and I knew it wasn't quite the right moment. I couldn't tell you what exactly made me feel that way. It was just a feeling. I had to trust that feeling.

Then that night, as I lay in bed ready to sleep, feeling all relaxed and calm, an idea popped into my head. I decided to reach out to someone I had met a while back. I don't know how or why this guy popped into my brain on a random Wednesday evening at 11 pm. But the next day I acted on it.

I had no clue what would come of it, where that idea came from or why it would even help.

That one conversation led to meetings and proposals, and it turned into a nearly £15,000 deal for me. My biggest one in a while. Life showed me the way!

On top of that, my connection back to the present moment gave me the energy to attend a new event.

I ended up connecting with someone who became a new paying financial coaching client. I'd previously been cancelling or not showing up for events because I was draining myself of all my excitement and energy and zest for life by how deeply I was in my head. I got stuck in a state of freeze, exhausted from the meaning I was making out of my situation and blocking myself from showing up in useful environments where stars could align.

I could never have imagined *how* I was going to solve my cash flow problem in my head. Instead, I got back to the present and into my body, and the ideas about where to go next flowed – and, before I knew it, my financial situation changed in a matter of weeks.

Only six weeks later, halfway into February 2025, I hit my quarterly target revenue goal of £20,000 for the business. This is not about manifesting, but about the magic of letting go to welcome in the present.

WHERE DO IDEAS COME FROM?

As busy humans in an overwhelming world, we all have moments like this where we are guided to places, people, situations, ideas, environments. . . but we ignore, miss or mistake them for something else.

Usually, we do this in favour of a louder, ego-led thought.

Maybe we convince ourselves our idea is stupid, pointless, scary, not the right time, etc. so we override our intuition and we act in alignment with our fearful thinking. And it's not until we look back and reflect (days, weeks or months later) and think '*I should have listened to my gut. The answer was there all along*'.

These ideas and insights come to us always in moments of presence and peace.

Our best ideas trickle into our bodies through the space between our thoughts – the beautiful silence of a present moment or the quiet that engulfs your entire being when you're in flow state.

There is something so magical about connecting to the present and letting the ideas come to us as opposed to force-thinking our way to a solution.

When you stop drowning out your intuition with the noise of thought, you can find peace in the present moment, and in this place of true presence your wisdom has the perfect runway to deliver ideas to you.

Peace is always there underneath all the noise of your thinking. It always has been, and it always will be.

You don't have to find peace or create new beliefs or add more thought to your life to change how you feel about money. It is a process of removal and unlearning.

When I had my own life-changing insight about this concept of letting thoughts fall away as opposed to adding more thought to find connection to the present moment, I remember this visual:

In your bedroom, if you removed all the furniture and decluttered the mess, there would just be space. Space is always there – you just add things into it. The furniture takes up room. But the space is always there. In fact, space has to be there for the furniture to have somewhere to go.

But when everything is removed, what's left? Space.

That is the same as peace.

Peace is space. The furniture is your thoughts. Peace has to be there for your thoughts to have a landing place.

When you let go of your judgements, your old beliefs and your stories – any thinking you have around money – what's left? Peace.

The peace beneath all the noise is where your wisdom lives.

We think that wisdom takes years to learn, but I don't agree with that sentiment. As I've shared many times throughout this book, you really are only one thought away from having a completely different life.

There are people who spend decades on this Earth but have no common sense and struggle with daily life. And there are young people who have such a strong connection to their own wisdom that they live a very happy and peaceful existence.

Near-death experiences can create sudden insights so profound that your entire life suddenly feels different even though nothing in reality has changed – people who survive car crashes often turn their entire life around and live happily not because their circumstances changed, but because one moment of clarity shifted their entire perspective.

And the magic? You don't need a traumatic event to have that shift. You can have a different experience of life almost immediately with one insight, one thought or one fresh perspective. With the knowledge that 'we are not our thoughts', letting your internal noise fall away and tapping into the wisdom underneath thought, the results can be instantly life-changing.

As humans, we instinctively know this is the best method: How many of us naturally believe in the concept of 'going for a walk to clear my mind' when you've been thinking too long on a problem? Your body knows it needs movement, nature and fresh environment to take you out of your head into your body and back into connection with yourself and the world.

The more we can focus on connecting to the present moment, the less stress and worry we feel about money. Not because our money problem disappears, but because we are not adding extra noise to the situation.

We are blocking our best ideas by overthinking. You do not solve a problem by thinking more but instead, by thinking less.

When you stop making up and believing stories about your situation, the less likely you are to sabotage your financial growth, and the more likely you are to listen to the sometimes simple, sometimes wild and sometimes seemingly unrelated ideas about what to do or where to go next.

You trust it is all part of the flow of life – everything is connected.

These ideas are coming from something greater than you. It is not your responsibility to create these ideas. Your job is to get present and lean into the flow of life, and then the bigger force at play will bring the creative ideas to you when you most need them. From that place it is only your responsibility to act upon them without judgement or needing to know how it'll all play out.

This is how so many artists create masterpieces, songwriters win Grammys and directors break box office records – because they create art from a connection to finding flow and letting the creativity move through them and out into the physical world.

In September 2025, I was nominated for 'Inspirational Women in the City 2025: The Champions' by *Brummell Magazine*, and I got to attend an art collection launch party. The artist, David Remfry, was asked *'What is your process behind creating your art?'*

He answered beautifully: *'It's not a conscious thing when I'm creating art. Something else is driving you. It's not "put-able" into words. It comes from inside in here'* *taps on his chest/stomach area* *'Whatever it is, it does not come with an intellectual starting point. It comes from an instinct. . .'*

As Remfry says, the magic of creation ALWAYS comes from something deeper and more profound (and unexplainable) than your thoughts. It is not your mind doing the work; it is your connection to the world where your best work comes from.

In this example, I am specifically referring to the creation of art, but the positive impact and beautiful consequence of being present extends way beyond just artistic creativity.

Our best ideas about what to do about a family problem, tough life decisions, etc. also come from a deeper, quieter place.

Presence is a beautiful place to find peace and comfort but also to receive ideas and connect to creativity.

WHY MORE FINANCIAL KNOWLEDGE WON'T CHANGE YOUR BEHAVIOUR

You do not find a new relationship with money in MORE information, thought or knowledge. You find it in peace, presence and connection.

I've hosted financial workshops at investment firms, banks and corporate offices with audiences of intelligent, bright and well-read individuals. And a similar pattern emerges every time: **Many people know what to do with their money; they just struggle to do it.**

They understand the basics of money management – spend less than you earn, save for emergencies and invest for the future. Yet they have a challenging time actually living by these principles, and their finances and well-being suffer as a result. Their knowledge says one thing, but their actions say something completely different.

If information alone were enough to create financial success, we'd all be wealthy by now.

We live in an age where financial knowledge is literally available at every corner you turn. We have AI tools like ChatGPT. We have 'FinFluencers' (myself included) sharing education across social media. Entire libraries of financial wisdom are accessible from your phone. The information is available, abundant and, nowadays, often free.

So the real questions are: Why don't we use it? Why do we gather all this information and then not execute it to the best of our ability?

Information does not directly correlate with action. Knowing something doesn't mean you'll behave in alignment with it. And money is not the only place this conflict occurs.

Let's compare it to your health:

We know the basics: Move your body; eat more vegetables than beige food; drink lots of water; exercise releases happy hormones; sleep is important; and sugar causes crashes. . .

So why do so many people struggle to implement healthy habits into their lives?

I want to tell you about my own experience when knowledge was not enough.

During my late teens and early twenties, I suffered (silently) from an eating disorder and a very poor relationship with food and my body.

At my worst, I became obsessed with information about health and nutrition. I devoured content on optimising health, analysing what was and wasn't good for my body. I followed fitness influencers, and I pinned healthy recipes on Pinterest. I tracked my food intake meticulously.

I basically did everything I could to fill my brain with 'good information'.

I was destroying my body one day at a time, oscillating between overeating and restriction, using exercise as punishment and treating food as comfort instead of fuel. I could have written an entire thesis on how to be a healthy young woman. And yet with all of that information, I struggled to confidently implement any sustainable habits or make choices aligned with who I desired to be.

The information was there in my brain, but none of my behaviour followed.

Reflecting on that time in my life, I'm aware that no amount of information was going to help me. It had to come from something much deeper.

Here is the thing: **Behaviour is feedback**. When there is a misalignment between what you know, what you want and how you behave, we are reminded that behaviour is never random. It is an indicator pointing us to something deeper. Your behaviour is simply reflecting what's happening inside of you at that moment in time.

I was very noisy inside and struggled to be present. Most of the time I was caught up in my own thoughts, judgement about myself, concerns about my future and all the other things that girls in their late teens/early twenties deal with.

I remember the day when I stopped extreme behaviours with eating. In a moment of pure silence and presence (which was not a regular occurrence), something inside of me said: '*This has to stop, this is not you, this is not who you are, this is not helping you in the way you think it is*'.

My wisdom had the opportunity to cut through the noise of thought, and it led me down an eight-year long period of self-recovery.

You might be thinking. . . '*Laura, it feels irresponsible to just live in the present moment all the time, it feels like I am avoiding my problems*'.

But you are not ignoring your problems, you are simply letting them be there. You're not running away from your problems, you're just giving them room to breathe and trusting that ideas will come to you in the calmer moments.

In Cal Newport's book, *Deep Work*, he writes about the power of letting the 'subconscious mind' go to work.

When you solve equations and maths problems, you first feed your brain with the variables for the situation, and then you leave it. You walk away, do something else and your brain goes to work to solve the problem, joining dots and making connections that your conscious logical brain cannot do.

On a deeper level, Einstein says: '*We cannot solve our problems with the same thinking we used when we created them*', highlighting how your thinking mind cannot find solutions to your situation, especially when your thinking is what created it. . .

The answer isn't more information. It's presence. It's getting quiet enough to let the wisdom underneath your thoughts come through. So, what do you actually need to make more aligned financial choices?

As I have shared, over the past few years, I invested five figures into retreats and 1:1 coaching in a new direction.

Now, I handle conflict and struggle in life in a completely different way. I no longer people-please or align with the notion of perfectionism. I'm not bogged down with the existential crisis that comes along with being a business owner.

And when it comes to my money, I have the most relaxed relationship with my finances ever.

Am I richer? More financially stable? Do I have more money in my bank account? Right now, no, not really. I've reinvested so much money back into the business, my mindset and my skill set that on paper, I'm not any 'richer'.

But my life is richer.

I am creating my own wealth in real time.

I trust my own abilities to grow my financial wealth, as I build wealth in all other areas.

Sometimes it happens simultaneously and sometimes it is a process. But finances are not scary or overwhelming like they used to be. I don't feel the pressure of society to be at a certain point with a certain amount, and it makes running a business way more enjoyable.

Will I be rich? Is that the aim? HELL YES, BABY. But I'm going to do my best to enjoy every step of the way. Even if that means growing my money at a slower pace.

And that is the power of understanding that you are not your thoughts. You are the peace beneath them. And from that place, anything is possible. And you can experience that peace by getting more present.

MEDITATION: A TOOL FOR PRACTISING PRESENCE

Something finally clicked for me about meditation, and it changed everything.

I yearned to be a daily meditator. Sometimes it brought me huge breakthroughs. But mostly it was super uncomfortable and was consumed by thoughts about work and my to-do list.

But then I learnt the point of meditation is not to stop having thoughts.

That's literally impossible. Thoughts happen. That is the nature of the mind. . . the *real* magic of meditation is learning to not react to your thoughts.

It doesn't require sitting cross-legged for hours in a perfectly quiet space or to have an extensive practice. You simply sit, breathe and notice your thoughts without immediately following them, judging them or reacting to them.

You learn presence, detachment and emotional regulation – three things that transform your relationship with everything, including money.

> 'Between stimulus and response there is space. In that space is our power to choose our response'.
>
> — *Viktor Frankl, Man's Search for Meaning*

Regular meditation has a real impact on your money because this space is where better financial decisions are made.

You start noticing the impulse to spend before you actually spend. You catch the thoughts 'I deserve a treat' or 'This will make me feel better'. Instead of instantly clicking 'Add to cart', you pause. You notice what is going on inside of you. Maybe it's stress, loneliness, comparison or a habit. Maybe you don't quite know. . .

But in that moment of noticing, you have a choice.

Of course, you can choose to still make the purchase – if it aligns with your desire, values or goals – but now you are making it consciously, not reactively.

Over time, these moments accumulate and transform your financial habits.

Benefits of meditation on your finances:

- **Less emotional spending:** You stop using shopping as a coping mechanism for uncomfortable feelings.
- **Less panic about money:** You can sit with financial discomfort without spiralling into the worst-case scenarios.
- **More intentional decisions:** You make choices based on your values and goals, not on impulse or fear.
- **More presence, less pressure:** You enjoy your life and money more because you're not constantly caught up in anxiety about the future or regret about the past.

A well-known Zen proverb goes: '*You should meditate for 20 minutes a day, unless you're too busy – then you should meditate for an hour*'.

Using lack of time as an excuse to avoid meditation is choosing your external world over your inner one. But this proverb reminds us: Nothing outside of you – not your financial wealth, job title, possessions or to-do list – truly matters if you're neglecting your world within.

The external will always demand more. Your inner world is where wisdom, clarity and peace live. The more you practise, the easier it becomes. And it's not a one-time event but an ever-evolving process and a way of being. You're training your brain and body to access the peace underneath the noise of thought, allowing you to build the financial life you truly want.

Head over to https://www.findyourwealthbook.com/resources to access a list of my favourite meditations. Whether you are starting out and need shorter guided meditations, or you are more advanced looking for new fresh tracks, all of my favourites are listed here!

Chapter 14

I – Imagine

Now you've let go of who you once were and released the attachment to old ways of thinking. You can start to dream up a new financial reality, a new way of being with money and find your version of wealth.

> 'Imagination is more important than knowledge. For knowledge is limited, whereas imagination embraces the entire world'.
>
> —*Albert Einstein*

Possibility lives inside your imagination; it creates this beautiful launching pad to step into the identity of someone who can hold wealth, create it and enjoy it. You can start asking yourself: 'What if?'.

Your imagination is the birthplace of your new reality.

Everything that exists in our physical world – every building, every invention, every business, every work of art – was first imagined in someone's mind. It started as a thought and it was brought to life in the external world. Your financial reality is no different.

To create a new financial reality, it can be beautiful to imagine it first. To see it, feel it and believe it's possible. And luckily, you don't need to know how it will happen, but you just need to know that it can be different, and that you get to create it!

In this chapter, I will be chucking questions at you like there is no tomorrow. Read them with an open and curious mind. There is no right or wrong answer to them, nor do you need to answer every single question. This is not the quiz show *Who Wants To Be a Millionaire*, where you only win the money if every answer is answered correctly.

I ask these questions as a way of opening your mind to possibility and to help you bring forth the answers in your heart and soul. This chapter is about dreaming big. . .

YOUR FINANCIAL VALUES

This first question that might make you squirm a little: **What do you actually value?**

Not what your parents told you to value. Not what you see all over Instagram and TikTok that makes you think you should want a capsule wardrobe, a minimalist apartment and a perfect morning routine. Not what society says success looks like or what your friends are doing or what that finance guru on YouTube says you need to prioritise.

Instead, consider what YOU actually value. What genuinely lights you up from the inside, what makes you feel most alive, most like yourself and most connected to what matters?

It is harder to build a financial life that feels good, aligned and that feels like it's actually yours, if you don't know what you're building it for in the first place.

Many people set financial goals because they think they should. Or they decide based on what they think they should want – the house, the six-figure salary, the investment portfolio and the early retirement – without ever stopping to ask if those things actually align with what makes them feel fulfilled and alive.

And then they wonder why achieving those goals feels empty, why getting the promotion didn't bring the satisfaction they expected or why buying the house felt more like checking a box than coming home to themselves.

So, let me ask you some questions, and I want you to sit with them, not just skim through looking for quick answers:

What experiences make you feel most alive? When have you felt that spark of aliveness – that sense of '*yes, this is what I'm here for*'? Was it whilst travelling? Creating something with your hands? Having a deep conversation that lasted for hours? Being in nature? Performing on stage? Teaching someone something new?

Your financial life should create more of whatever lights you up, not less of it.

When do you feel most like yourself? Not the version of yourself you think you should be, not the persona you put on for work or for social media, but the real, truest version of you.

Because money, when used well, should allow you to be more of yourself, not force you into being someone you're not.

What would you do if money were no object? Although cliché, there's a reason why people keep asking it: The answer reveals what you actually care about when all external pressures and limitations are stripped away. If money were completely irrelevant and if you had enough to cover everything, how would you spend your days? What would you create? Who would you spend time with? What problems would you try to solve?

The gap between your current life and that answer shows you where your values might not be reflected in how you're actually living.

If you had 24 hours left to live, what would actually matter? Strip away everything else – the career goals, the financial targets, the material possessions, the achievements and the status symbols. If you knew you only had one more day, what would you want to spend it doing? Who would you want to be with? What would you want to say?

Those answers reveal your core values with brutal clarity, and when time is limited, we naturally prioritise what actually matters vs. what we've been told should matter.

You might start to notice an uncomfortable gap between those values and how you're currently living, including how you're using money. Remember: We notice but we don't judge.

Maybe you value freedom and adventure, but you're working 60-hour weeks to afford a house you barely spend time in because you thought that's what you were supposed to do at your age.

Maybe you value creativity and self-expression, but you've been so focused on saving every penny that you haven't bought art supplies or taken that pottery class.

Maybe you value relationships and deep connection, but you're so stressed about money you never have the bandwidth to be fully present with the people you love or you've been saying no to social events and trips away.

The gap between what you say you value and how you're actually allocating your resources, including your money, is where a lot of financial dissatisfaction lives.

It's why you can be doing everything 'right' according to conventional financial wisdom and still feel like something is missing, still feel unfulfilled and still feel like the money you're making, saving and investing isn't actually creating the life you want to live.

There is no need to feel guilty about this gap if it exists. The goal is simply to see it clearly, to acknowledge it without judgement and then to start making different choices moving forward.

Now let's talk about the role money plays in your life. Once you have some clarity on your actual values, the next question becomes: **What role do you want money to play?**

Do you want it to buy you time? Time to create, time with your family, to rest, to think and to pursue projects that don't have an immediate financial return, but that feed your soul?

Do you want it to buy you freedom? Freedom to say no to misaligned work, freedom to take risks and try new things without the fear of financial ruin and freedom to make choices based on what feels right rather than what pays the bills?

Do you want it to buy you experiences? Travel to places that expand your perspective, courses and workshops that help you grow, concerts, art and theatre that move you, meals with people you love, or adventures that become stories you tell for the rest of your life?

Do you want it to buy you impact? The ability to support causes you care about, to help people in your community, to fund solutions to problems that break your heart and to leave the world a little better than you found it?

There's no wrong answer here. Nor is there a definitive definition you *have* to give it.

A PRACTICAL EXERCISE WITH YOUR MONEY

A client once told me she really valued health and wanted to shop at farmers' markets each weekend, buying bone broth, fresh fruit, punnets of wild mushrooms and ingredients that make you glow from the inside out. These ingredients do not come at the same price point as your standard packaged food you find in a big supermarket. She said: '*I know I can't afford that yet. I will just have to wait until I have more money I guess. . .*'

Interestingly, when assessing her spending over the previous months, we found she had actually been spending approximately £200 a month on fast food, but she was none the wiser. All of those little purchases added up to so much money – enough to do a small weekly shop at a farmers' market, the very thing she so badly desired and said she valued.

Instead of beating herself up for 'wasting money', she seized the opportunity to shift her behaviours. This was her chance to bring herself closer to her desired lifestyle – a dream she thought wasn't possible for a few years, not until her business started making more money.

Each week she would go to the farmers' market and spend the small amount of money she had saved throughout the week (by intentionally not spending on convenience food), and the impact was amazing. Even though she couldn't do her full weekly shop yet, the small act completely changed her energy, health and attitude.

Before she knew it, from this place of alignment and intention, she was embodying the wealthiest version of herself, and her business sales started increasing too.

All of this was possible by understanding her values and then seeing how her current financial behaviour aligned with them.

A year later, she emailed to say she does her full shop at the farmers' market. Instead of waiting for that reality to magically appear someday, the combination of awareness, acceptance and a choice to live more in alignment with her values made this reality possible.

If you don't know where your money goes each month and you've convinced yourself you don't have enough to spend money on the things you truly value – try looking back over your spending.

What do your current purchases say about you? Where can you get more intentional with your spending to start to create the reality you want?

Even if you have to start small, your values can become a guiding light towards the full reality you desire.

YOUR FINANCIAL GOALS

Are your goals actually yours? This is the first question you need to ask yourself, and it's not always an easy one to answer honestly.

A lot of people think that their biggest financial goal is to buy a house.

In the United Kingdom, people are obsessed with buying property. Back in the 1960s and 1970s, when house prices aligned with the average salary in each region, buying property was an incredible investment, providing both a home to live in and a financial foundation to build on – paying off your mortgage so your money compounds. By retirement, you have a house with no mortgage (reducing your monthly outgoings). Or you own an asset that has (hopefully) gone up in price, allowing you to sell the house, downsize and make a profit – an ideal set-up.

But now, in the 2020s, as many young people or first-time buyers know, the housing market is very different. Buying property is harder, the entry price point is higher, houses are overvalued and the market is more volatile.

And I'm not against owning property – it can be great for the right person at the right time. But there's a massive difference between wanting a house because you think you should, or have been told you need to, vs. wanting to buy a house because it's a dream to call a place your own and to create a space of comfort and safety, regardless of what anyone else thinks.

When I had £25,000 in savings, its initial purpose was to go travelling (then COVID-19 hit), so that money sat there. . . waiting for a new purpose. I wasn't stressed about it, and I knew purpose can shift over time or when new opportunities are presented to you. Yet everyone told me I should buy a house. But everything inside of me was like: '*Ew, I don't want to be tied to one location. I don't want a mortgage. I don't need a house. The world is my home*'.

I am a Sagittarius rising sign with a lot of 5 in my numerology (the number for adventure!), so I deeply value travel. Exploring lights me up, so buying a home made no sense to my soul. Luckily, I listened to that voice inside telling me it wasn't right to get on the property ladder.

So, I need you to get really honest with yourself about whether your goals are coming from you because not all goals are equal and actually yours.

When everyone has ideas about what your goals should be, all of that noise can make it really hard to hear what you actually want.

The 'should' trap is real. '*I should save up for a house*'. '*I should have £10,000 in an emergency fund*'. '*I should retire early*'. All of these 'shoulds' might be perfectly good goals for someone, but are they good goals for you?

So, some questions to ask yourself about your current financial goals:

Do I want this or do I think I should want this? Be brutally honest. If you're pursuing something primarily because you think it's what you're supposed to do at your age or in your position, that's a red flag. Sound the alarm!

Would I still want this if no one knew about it? If the goal loses its appeal when you imagine achieving it in complete privacy, with no one to impress or prove anything to, then it might not be your goal, and it might be more about external validation than internal satisfaction.

Does this align with *my* values or someone else's? Go back to the values you identified in the section above. Does this goal support what matters to me? Or is it supporting someone else's version of success?

Am I chasing this to prove something? Sometimes our financial goals are more about proving we're successful, worthy or 'good enough' than they are about creating a life we want to live.

Once you've identified goals that feel genuinely yours, the next step is to get underneath them. Because the goal itself is rarely the real goal – the feeling underneath is what you're actually after.

Don't just ask what you want but also ask why you want it.

Discovering what feeling you're actually chasing helps you to get creative about how to access that feeling, which might change the specific goals you set or how you pursue them.

Also, from everything you have learnt so far, you now know that you can create those feelings (of security, safety, excitement, adventure and joy) inside yourself – before you have even reached your goal!

What actually excites you? Not '*what should I be saving for?*', but '*what lights me up when I think about it?*' There's a difference between goals that feel like obligations and goals that genuinely excite you.

The energy test is simple: Does thinking about this goal drain you or energise you? If thinking about saving for a house makes you feel heavy and trapped, but thinking about saving for a year of travel makes you feel alive and inspired, that's information you shouldn't ignore.

And really it could change again in any moment, but you have to start somewhere!

If you are struggling to get clear answers on these questions, that's no problem. The answers will reveal themselves over time as you get more aware and more present. Your goals don't have to look responsible or impressive to anyone else – as long as they feel true to you!

Head over to https://www.findyourwealthbook.com/resources for my Financial Values and Goals masterclass where I take this even deeper and help you embed these into your financial life.

A PERMISSION SLIP TO WANT MORE MONEY

I would like to shout this one from the rooftops: It's okay to want more money.

There's a societal belief that wanting money makes us evil or greedy or selfish. That if you're conscious or a good person, you shouldn't care about money. That wanting nice things or financial success is somehow shallow or unspiritual.

But wanting nice things, beautiful experiences, financial security and abundance is not bad – not bad at all. Remember, you get to choose the meaning you attach to money.

It is okay to desire a financially successful life and to own that and go after it with a relaxed whimsy, an open mind and a sense of possibility. In fact, it is more than okay, and I encourage it. Discover what you want and why you want it, go after it with excitement, intention and sometimes what can feel like delusion.

A social media trend in 2025 was '*delulu is the solulu*'. . . the translation is 'being delusional is the solution'. I am a huge advocate for permission to dream BIG – to let yourself want what you want without immediately shutting it down as impossible or impractical or too much.

When I decided I wanted to go to Drama School but had absolutely no way of funding my dream, I had to be a little bit delusional. I needed £15,000 as a minimum. I got no help from family or friends. I was 19 on a £12,000 salary. If I tried to be 'realistic' with my goals, I never would have even started saving any money.

My attitude was '*I have this goal, I know I can achieve it, I don't know how, but let's give it a go*'.

Don't be afraid to be 'delusional' about your financial dreams. You never know where you could end up. I truly believe we were all given our desires for a reason, and shaming yourself for wanting more money or a different financial reality only keeps you stuck.

> 'Shoot for the moon. Even if you miss, you'll land among the stars'.
>
> —*Norman Vincent Peale*

Now, let's be clear about when wanting money becomes dangerous because there is a line that you don't want to cross.

When money becomes your *everything* – the only thing you think about, the only measure of success you care about and the only goal worth pursuing – that's when it becomes a problem. Sacrificing your peace, health, relationships and joy in pursuit of it is a slippery slope. Tying your self-worth to your net worth gives too much power to money.

But wanting more money while also valuing your peace, wanting financial success while also maintaining your relationships and your joy, and wanting wealth while knowing it doesn't define your worth. All of that is wisdom!

I talk about approaching your financial goals with 'relaxed whimsy' – moving towards what you want without gripping it so tightly that you strangle the life out of it. I promise you it is possible to desire more money and still enjoy your life right now.

And finally, do not forget to own your desire fully.

There is power in claiming what you want without shame, without apology, without making yourself smaller to make other people more comfortable.

When you own your own desires unapologetically, it actually inspires people to do the same. You become a shining light for others, an expander for the people around you and a role model to those who can't yet feel it for themselves.

When I started to own my financial desires, the people around me felt safe to do the same. It has been such a beautiful journey to watch my friends and family do the same. I have watched friends pull themselves out of debt, start building their own safety net and chasing their dreams. You can influence up and down: My mum and my sister, Beth, have both owned their desires and created new financial realities for themselves, and I am so proud of them. It makes me emotional thinking about it.

When you own your own desires, you help not only yourself but the people around you.

And for those people around you who judge you, shame you or try to '*pull you back down to Earth*', know that they are only viewing your actions through their own thinking about money. It has nothing to do with what you are doing and everything to do with how they are thinking about what you are doing.

'*People think you're crazy until you're successful*' – many successful individuals say they have experienced the onslaught of judgement from others when they are delusional and go after their goals. But the moment it all clicks into place and works, people change their mind about what you have achieved and how you have done it.

If someone is not yet ready to own their own desires and go after them, that is not your responsibility. Let them have their opinions, and maybe when you have achieved your version of wealth and they see you living a happy, fulfilled and healthy life, they will want to do the same.

And whilst not your responsibility to change their thinking, this book would make a great Christmas present for anyone who is struggling. . .

MONEY AS AN AMPLIFIER

There's this pervasive belief that money changes people, that it turns good people bad and that wealth inevitably leads to greed or selfishness or losing yourself. But that's not actually what happens.

We probably can all name a handful of extremely wealthy people on this planet who are doing awful things (that we would never do if we had their level of financial resource). But at the same time, there are just as many people out there with a lot of money doing incredible things with their financial resources.

When financial constraints are removed – when you physically have more money, more resources and more options – your true essence gets amplified. I like to think more money lets you just be more of you!

If someone is generous with little money, more resources usually widen that generosity. They give more, help more and create more impact because giving is already part of who they are.

If someone is controlling with little money, more money gives them more to control, more to micro-manage and more ways to try to force outcomes because the need for control was already there.

Money acts as a psychological spotlight that illuminates what's running underneath, which is why doing the inner work matters so much, and why I'm spending so much time in this book on awareness, acceptance, letting go and getting present.

Money amplifies more of who you already are. When you nurture your own inner world so who you truly are can blossom, money becomes a beautiful tool and not a dangerous weapon.

Chapter 15

G – Guide Your Mind

> 'The most common way people give up their power is by thinking they don't have any'.
>
> —*Alice Walker*

Now that you have explored your desire, values and goals, the role you'd like money to play in your life and have dreamed up a potential new and exciting financial future, it is time to ask the question: *How do you actually use your mind as a tool to create the life you want?*

The previous three chapters highlighted that we are not our thoughts, living in the present without identifying with every thought that happens to us and imagining a new financial reality. This chapter is about intentionally guiding your mind by harnessing the power of thought.

USING MANTRAS EFFECTIVELY

I have a love–hate relationship with mantra work. . .

Most people use mantras because they want to change their reality. They want to become a new version of themselves and shift from where they are to where they want to be.

Some people swear by them, crediting affirmations with changing their entire life. Other people roll their eyes and say they're useless. Standing in front of a mirror and saying 'I am wealthy' when you're struggling to pay bills feels ridiculous and changes nothing. Their effectiveness really depends on how you're using them.

The assumption seems to be that if you repeat 'I am wealthy, I am abundant and I am successful' enough times, then your reality will magically shift to match those words. And when it inevitably doesn't work, they either think they're doing something wrong, they decide mantras are bullshit or they double down and say them even more, hoping that eventually the words will become true.

But that's not how this works.

Let's go back to the basics: Thought creates feeling, and feeling drives action. Which means that for a mantra to actually *change* anything, it has to create a real feeling inside of you.

It has to shift your current state of being. If the words you're saying don't generate any genuine emotion, if they're just empty sounds you're repeating robotically, they're pointless. They're not doing anything except maybe making you feel silly.

If you're standing in front of the mirror saying '*I am so rich, I have so much money, abundance flows to me effortlessly*' while part of you is thinking '*LOL I have £10 in my account and bills to pay*', you just feel like you are lying to yourself.

So, the first thing to note is that the feeling matters. The mantra has to land in your body and create an actual emotional shift for it to have any power.

But I want to take it one layer deeper. . .

The other thing you will have learned throughout this book: Emotions are transient. They move through you. Your mood always shifts naturally throughout the day. You never stay in one emotion for the entire day – or at least you can't expect yourself to.

It means saying some mantras in the morning and then hoping you'll remain in a 'high vibe state' all day long, and that *all* of your actions will flow from that elevated place. That's asking a lot from a mantra.

It is not realistic!

So, if mantras can't keep you in an elevated state all day, and if just repeating words without feeling doesn't do anything, then what are they actually for?

The last thing you want is to feel that, for mantras to work, you have to say them multiple times throughout the day. . . if every time you found yourself in a low mood, you thought 'QUICK START REPEATING MANTRAS. I NEED TO RAISE MY VIBE!!!'

A few years back, in a bid to change my own reality, I had a period of my life where my mantra routine looked like repeating them every hour on the hour. Surely, the more times I say them, the more likely they are to work? I was desperate. And it's no surprise that it didn't do anything, except take up my time and clog up my brain.

If you want to change your current reality, remember that EVERYTHING is happening in the now – always and forever. The only moment we have *is* now – the present moment.

So, that means you can become a new version of yourself in the now, in this very moment. You don't have to wait for some future date when you finally 'arrive' at your new desired reality.

Instead, the aim is to act like that version of yourself right now, making choices in the now that reflect this new reality.

Think about the version of you that has everything you want. If you had everything you already wanted in life (abundance of money, thriving relationships, a fit and healthy body and a sense of purpose) and you had reached a state of '*I am happy with my life exactly as it is*', do you think you would still be using mantras to create a new reality?

Would that version of you be walking around all day saying affirmations, trying desperately to convince themselves that they're wealthy and rich and happy?

No, of course not.

Because you would already BE it. It would already be your normal baseline reality.

You wouldn't need to convince yourself of anything because you would already be living it. You would naturally be in a state of gratitude, joy, abundance and wealth. There would be no need to force it or perform it because at that moment it is already happening.

So, if your future wealthiest self isn't spending their entire day repeating affirmations, then why would you do that?

You don't use mantras to convince yourself of something that isn't true. Instead, you can use mantras as a reminder to act like your future self in the now.

They are a simple reminder in the moment to drop back into presence and ask yourself: '*Who am I being right now? Am I being the version of me who's stressed and panicking about money, or am I being the version of me who's calm and confident and grateful?'*

A mantra isn't a magic spell that changes your external reality. It's a tool that helps you embody your future identity right now, in this moment, with this choice.

When you say 'I am wealthy', or 'I am abundant', or 'Money flows to me easily', you're not trying to convince yourself that your bank account is overflowing when it's not.

You're reminding yourself to feel and act the way your future self – who does have financial abundance – would feel and act. And there is no doubt that version of you would be feeling grateful, present and at peace.

It brings us to why mantras need to work hand in hand with gratitude.

THE POWER OF GRATITUDE

Gratitude gets a bad rap because it's often taught as toxic positivity. *'Just be grateful for what you have and stop wanting more!'* As if wanting to improve your life and being grateful for where you are now are mutually exclusive.

You can be deeply and genuinely grateful for what you have right now AND still want more. You can appreciate where you are AND work towards where you want to be.

The wealthiest version of you who has everything they want will just be so grateful. . .

When you practise genuine gratitude – when you wake up and actually feel grateful for where you are, and when you look at your current life through the lens of appreciation rather than lack – you're training your brain to look for what's good.

If you say '*I have so much to be grateful for, there's so much good in my life already, and I'm supported and abundant in ways I haven't even fully acknowledged*', your mind will get to work looking for evidence of THAT.

You'll notice the money that does come in. The opportunities that are available. The resources you already have. The ways you're actually already wealthy – maybe not in the bank account but in relationships, health, experiences, skills, time and freedom.

When you start noticing what's good and when you start seeing abundance that's already here, you feel differently. So, from THAT place you will act differently and you will make different choices from a genuine sense of already having enough. . . which paradoxically creates more!

This is why mantras work so beautifully alongside gratitude.

COMBINING MANTRAS WITH GRATITUDE

Waking up and robotically repeating '*I am abundant, I am abundant, I am abundant*' a hundred times while feeling absolutely nothing (or worse, while feeling the inner conflict of knowing your bank account is low) is a recipe for feeling worse.

But if you wake up, take a moment to feel genuine gratitude for what is already there: Maybe it's the warm bed you're lying in. The roof over your head. The fact that your body woke up today. The coffee you're about to make. The friend who texted you yesterday. The fact that you have the capacity to read this book.

They are all things to feel genuinely grateful for.

And from that place of real gratitude, if you say a mantra such as '*I am wealthy, I am grateful, and wealth flows to me*', then guess what happens? What you are saying is now actually true.

It's because you *are* grateful. You are experiencing a form of wealth – maybe not financial abundance yet but emotional wealth, relational wealth, the wealth of being alive and having another day to create and grow and experience life.

The mantra isn't trying to convince you of something. It's affirming something you're actually feeling at this moment.

And that feeling – that genuine state of gratitude and abundance – is exactly how your future self, the one with the overflowing bank account, would feel.

It's not because of money, but because your wealthiest future self naturally sees abundance, notices what's good and feels grateful for what they have.

You're not waiting to feel that way until you have more money. You're feeling that way NOW, which in turn makes you become the person who creates and attracts more.

You're looking at your current life through the lens of someone who is already wealthy and grateful for what they have and not '*I'll be grateful when I have all these nice things*'. But '*I'm grateful now. I love these elements of my life now. I appreciate what's here now*'.

So, yes, sure, use mantras as a tool (IF that works for you!). But use them as anchors, not as magic spells.

- Use them in the morning as a way to instantly drop into gratitude and presence before your day begins.
- Use them before you make a financial decision as a reminder: '*Who am I being at this moment? Am I making this choice from my old identity or my new one?*'
- Use them before bed as a way to close down your day from a place of genuine gratitude rather than worry or panic.

But don't use them as a way to convince yourself of something you don't believe. Don't repeat them robotically without any feeling. Don't expect them to keep you in an elevated state 24/7 without any other work.

Instead, pair them with genuine gratitude and presence. Act like your future self in this moment. Do not wait until some distant future to embody who you're becoming because your wealthiest self is not constantly affirming their abundance. They're just living it, waking up grateful and moving through the day noticing what is good.

And you can do that right now with whatever you have in your bank account or whatever circumstances you're in.

VISUALISATION: SEEING A NEW REALITY

Visualisation is the process of training your brain to see possibilities, to familiarise yourself with the feeling of your desired reality and to create a clear enough picture that your actions start naturally aligning with that vision.

Visualisation works because your brain doesn't know the difference between what you vividly imagine in your mind and what you experience in reality. We already know this from the work we've done on understanding how thought creates your experience.

Thought happens in your mind first – everything you experience is filtered through your thinking. So, if thought creates your experience, you can use your mind to guide your thoughts to create a feeling and to be in control of directing your own behaviour.

Athletes are the most well-known and open about using visualisation as a tool to improve their performance. It is why actors rehearse scenes in their mind and why surgeons mentally walk through complex procedures before performing them.

> 'I use visualisation a lot. I try to see the ball going where I want it to go'.
>
> —*Novak Djokovic*

Michael Phelps attributed a lot of his swimming success to the process of 'mental videotapes' (aka visualisation). His coach, Bob Bowman, would get him to rehearse his races in his mind in extreme detail – the rhythm of his strokes, the feel of the water, the noise of the crowd, the turns and the finish – and even more interestingly, he would also visualise things going wrong, such as a poor start or his goggles filling with water.

At the 2008 Beijing Olympics, during the 200m butterfly final, Phelps' goggles filled with water after the dive. He could barely see, but instead of panicking, he relied entirely on his internal 'mental videotape' and went on to win gold and set a world record. How cool is that?

There are countless successful people sharing their mental processes around guiding the mind to create the feeling of winning before it happens, mentally rehearsing the good, the bad and the ugly so the body knows how to react to each scenario and creating mental resilience so that they are always prepared.

When you visualise something clearly and repeatedly, you're building familiarity, reducing resistance and making that future reality feel more possible and accessible. But you're not just trying to see a picture in your mind. You're trying to feel what it would be like to be living that reality. The feeling is the most important part.

Visualisation is not only to imagine yourself winning or to react quickly and calmly in times of uncertainty when something has gone wrong, but also sometimes to prepare yourself to bounce back and recover from failure.

You can use it as a tool to help shape your character.

Serena Williams – one of the greatest athletes of all time with 23 Grand Slams – knows not only about the power of the mind when it comes to winning but also the extreme importance of behaviour as a role model in sports and public-facing influence. She says '*A champion is defined not by their wins but by how they can recover when they fall*'.

We have seen time and time again, on TV and through the media, the attention athletes receive when they behave with outrage, struggling to maintain their own anger about a situation such as losing.

Learning how to maintain a cool temperament and manage your own emotional reactions shows mental discipline and can be achieved through guiding the power of your mind.

My wonderful friend Maya Raichoora has written a book called *Visualise: Think, Feel, Perform Like the Top 1%* – an entire book on this process of using mental imagery which I highly recommend if you want to get serious about your visualising.

Practising Visualisation

You should settle into a meditative state (you can be anywhere when you visualise), close your eyes, take a few deep breaths and start to create the mental imagery in your mind.

Now, imagine the version of you who has the financial reality you desire. It's not just about the money in the bank but also the whole experience. And it's also about the relationship with money, the confidence, the ease and the freedom.

See them clearly: How do you carry yourself? What does your morning routine look like? How do you dress – not because appearance matters but because how you dress often reflects how you feel about yourself. What does your home look like? What environment have you created for yourself? What does your workday look like?

Feel into your experience: How do you feel when you wake up? What's your energy like throughout the day? How do you feel when you check your bank account? What's your baseline emotional state around money? Is there peace? Confidence? Excitement? Calm?

Notice your actions: How do you make financial decisions? What do you do when an unexpected expense comes up? How do you spend money? Save money? Give money? How do you talk about money? How do you handle stress or uncertainty?

Spend time with this version of yourself. Get to know them. Make them vivid and real in your mind.

And then – and this is the important part – ask them: 'What would you do in my situation right now? What advice do you have for me? What do you see that I'm missing? What would you want me to know?'

Listen and see what comes up. Your future self has wisdom for you, and they're more accessible than you think.

Boom – the visualisation is complete.

The more real it feels in your mind, the more naturally you'll start acting in ways that align with it, and when your actions align with your vision, your external reality begins to shift.

Head over to https://www.findyourwealthbook.com/resources to access a set of financial visualisation audio tracks that will help you create your new desired financial reality.

Customising Visualisation

I have something called Aphantasia.

> *Definition: Aphantasia is a neurological variation, often called 'mind blindness', characterised by the inability to voluntarily create mental images in one's mind.*

Essentially, I cannot create clear mental imagery in my mind. When I close my eyes, I only see black. If you ask me to 'visualise' something specific, I cannot see it, but I can feel it. I cannot see colours or shapes or patterns.

Apparently, only 2–5% of the world's population has this condition.

A few years ago, as I aimlessly doomscrolled on TikTok, a video popped up explaining this. At first, it made me sad – I couldn't believe that other people were having full visual experiences in life every single day. It made me feel like I was missing out.

But I experience the world in a different way. I 'visualise' through feeling. And it's one of the key elements of using mental imagery – to create a feeling. So if, like me, you have this experience of the world, do not stress. You can still use this tool, but you just have to use it in your own way.

Even though I cannot 'see' in my mind's eye, I can still dream at night-time. And I have a heightened sense of sound. Music is very emotional for me; it can move me to tears and make me feel every emotion under the sun, and I have a very physical reaction to sound. So, I use music to create an experience inside myself, and then I walk through my own movie using thought and feeling, and that does the job for me!

So, if this is you, do not fret – we are in this together! Find your own version of visualisation. . . or, if it's not for you, don't use it at all. You should do whatever works for you and your life.

Chapter 16

N – Navigate with Aligned Action

> 'Life shrinks or expands in proportion to one's courage'.
>
> —*Anaïs Nin*

Abundance is not some random woo-woo mindset – it is a way of living. You can view the world differently in an instant, and I hope you've had your own experience of 'nothing has changed, but everything is different' throughout the book.

This is where the 'practical work' comes in because creating the financial reality you desire requires movement, action, momentum. . . and living your life!

I once read *A Mystical Girl in a Material World* by Ruby Warrington – it's an explorative guide to the modern-day woman discovering a deeper connection to the universe, blending spirituality modalities with 21st-century living. Each chapter shared information on topics such as tarot, astrology, crystals, chakras, etc. It was a beginner manual with tools that *might* elevate my life, without forcing them down my throat in a cult-like approach.

Fascinated by the astrology section, I stayed up until 6 am learning to read my chart and began to embed it into my life gently. I was excited to implement what I'd learnt in my own way, without feeling the need to live by it religiously.

I would love for you to approach this chapter of the book with the same approach: '*take what resonates, leave what doesn't*'. We'll explore practical ways to implement this work into your daily life, and how you can sustainably stay connected to what you've learnt in this book.

COMPARING THE WHEEL OF LIFE

A common belief is 'effort equals outcome'. Working hard increases your chance of achieving your desired outcome. And that forcing and pushing hard enough to integrate every new tool or behaviour into your life ensures the promise of a specific life.

As the popular expression goes, '*If hard work led to success, the donkey would own the farm*'.

Let's shift our focus from effort to ease – not from *doing* less but from doing *differently – from doing to being* and understanding what ease can look like and the beautiful impact it has.

Think about an area of your life that feels easy to you. Maybe your career has always felt easy: never in a period of unemployment even when employment levels are down, promotions come easy, pay rises are handed to you and your work is recognised by senior management.

What approach do you take to this successful area of your life? What is your thinking? How do you behave?

Usually the answer is: '*I don't really think about it, it just happens. It flows with ease*'.

You naturally act without much thought in that area of your life and yet things beautifully fall into place somehow. . . it feels natural and doesn't require much force. You are just being you, showing up, being present and things work out.

Well, money is no different. You can live your life with the same amount of ease and flow in your financial life if you 'apply' the same approach and energy.

Let me share an example of two areas of my life: One that has flowed with ease and the other that has been a struggle for me.

Romantic Relationships

I always struggled with romantic relationships.

I was single until the age of 31 – I had no 'proper' relationship. I dated in the past but struggled to get past the second date. I always thought *'Ugh why does this always happen to me?'*

I used to believe *'I cannot trust men; intimacy is scary, I'm not confident with romance and it is hard to find a relationship'*. When I was younger, I unfortunately had some awful experiences with men so it made sense where this thinking originated. But as you can imagine, through this lens, all my romantic encounters repeatedly followed this trajectory. I felt doomed in love.

'I don't think I will ever fall in love', I told my therapist at 26.

For every romantic interaction, I prepared for the worst, expecting it to take the same path as all the others.

Then when inevitably it did, I made each 'failed' experience mean something about me – a loop I didn't realise I was creating and was stuck in.

In 2022, as I started my business, I met one of my best friends Nina. Her attitude towards dating was SO refreshing and I went on a new dating journey with her by my side. Everything changed. Without force, I listened to myself and my reality shifted with it. Dating was fun again – I stopped overthinking any romantic interaction or letting my singleness be a reflection of who I am or what is to come. I realised that, just like with friends, there are an abundance of people I could date. People come and go, and everything is a lesson or an experience.

In September 2024, I attended a mindfulness retreat and transitioned from embodying 'I am unlovable' to 'I am love'. Not as a mantra repeated in front of the mirror or a practice around self-love, but I chose to drop the attachment to my old way of thinking about love. I chose to think about it less and to let fresh ideas come through.

Only a few weeks later, I met the man I fell in love with. My new sense of ease around romantic relationships allowed me to navigate this experience in a completely different way. From believing I'd be single forever, I chose to welcome in one of the most beautiful, expansive experiences.

Friendships

Ever since I was a child, I've been amazing at making friends. Beautiful new connections have popped up seemingly out of nowhere, and I have made friends throughout every walk of my life.

My attitude towards friendships feels abundant. Anyone could be a friend, yet I am discerning who I become friends with. I learnt how to trust my own intuition on letting friends go, knowing that I am making the right decision to move on from a friendship. I know and trust that every friend is for a reason, a season or a lifetime. I am a good home for friendship to blossom, the ones who are meant to be in my life will stay and those who aren't will fall away.

I am not codependent on my best friends, nor do I put everything on them. This is not an area of my life I have had to make a conscious, strained effort with – which is not to say I don't make an effort with my friendships. In fact, it's quite the opposite. But the effort I put into my friendships feels effortless.

I'm not perfect. I have made mistakes in friendships, but I learn from them. I've made decisions to walk away from friends who made me feel shit, disrespected me, drained my cup. . . trusting that whether my circle was small or big, I will be okay. I embodied the understanding that friendships ebb and flow.

When comparing romantic relationship and friendships, one felt easy and one felt hard. Both taught me something.

Changing my approach to love showed me how I could change anything in life. And my lifelong approach to friendship was a great reference point – There was no more force, applying unnecessary pressure or pushing desperately for change.

As I thought less about money and more about living my life, my relationship with it naturally changed and finally felt easy. And this is possible for you too.

HAVING FUN

> 'Sometimes the most spiritual thing you can do is have fun'.
>
> —*Gabby Bernstein*

The self-help world can get you absorbed in prioritising 'bettering yourself'. So, it can be easy to get caught up on 'improving yourself', constantly working on yourself.

But that narrative can keep you stuck and isolated if you don't actually get out into the world and have experiences.

If all you ever do is work on yourself, you're not actually living. You're preparing to live. And life is happening right now, not once you've finally become the perfect version of yourself.

Life is meant to be fun and enjoyed – not endured, optimised or turned into a relentless self-improvement project but really, truly and wonderfully enjoyed.

There is no prize at the end of your life for suffering through things that could have been changed.

Let me tell you about two of my favourite things: laughing and dancing.

Laughing: The Podcast That Saved Me

One time, deep in the thick of 'doing all this work on myself', I was so focused on healing that I'd forgotten how it felt to just enjoy myself.

On a walk, I wanted to listen to a podcast. My immediate thought was: *'I should listen to something where I'm learning or growing. Something productive that helps me move forward'*.

And then I caught myself in that thinking and I stopped in the street. I got quiet and listened to myself. Instead of following what I thought I should be doing, I instead asked myself, *'What do I want right now?'*

My immediate answer was: I want to laugh.

So I put on the *Good Hang Podcast* with Amy Poehler and then went to *Off Menu* with Ed Gamble and James Acaster (specifically the episode with Sue Perkins, which if you haven't listened to, stop what you're doing and go listen right now). Suddenly I found myself absolutely howling with laughter and I felt lighter than I had in weeks.

Not everything has to be in service of bettering yourself or moving you forward. Sometimes the best thing you can do – the most healing, the most transformative and the most spiritual thing – is stop trying to fix yourself and just have fun. Whatever fun means to you.

Because when you're laughing so hard your stomach hurts or dancing until your feet ache, fully present in the moment of pure enjoyment, you're not worried about money, anxious about the future or replaying past mistakes over like a movie in your mind. You're just here, alive and experiencing joy.

And that is the point. Not a distraction, but being here and creating your own joy.

When I realised there is 'no inherent meaning' to life and that you get to make meaning out of your own life, I was initially devastated. *'WHAT DO YOU MEAN I HAVE NO PURPOSE? What am I supposed to do? What's the point of any of this?'*

But as the dust settled, something shifted. 'Oh. Wait. That's actually. . . fun? How freeing'.

If there's no predetermined purpose for life or no specific way I'm meant to live my life, then I get to decide. I get to choose what matters to me and how I want to spend my time.

What a beautiful shift in the way you approach life.

Think about playing board games. Most of the time, there's a clear objective: a way to complete it, a way to win and a way to succeed. Essentially, you are working towards a specific outcome.

Now think of *The Sims*. There is no end point where you've 'beaten' the game. The actual fun is in the playing of the game: creating a life for your character, making choices and seeing what happens.

This is the same as life.

The fun is in the playing! – the living, the experiencing and the experimenting. It's not in reaching some final destination where you've 'won' at life or become the perfect version of yourself or achieved all your goals. It would be boring if we were all the same. The beauty is in the diversity of experience, in the different ways we each choose to play.

One of my favourite books *Die with Zero* by Bill Perkins talks about the concept of 'memory dividends'. I audibly gasped when the message he was conveying sank in – the insight I had was so groundbreaking that it stayed with me ever since.

> 'Remember: In the end, the business of life is the acquisition of memories'.
>
> —*Bill Perkins*

Memories you create throughout life continue to pay emotional rewards for years to come. That's the importance of not saving up all your fun for later in life. . . you'd have no stories to tell or good memories to enrich your life!

This book vocalised my own experience in life: **Money is powerful, but the true return on investments is in how you live.** And this requires being open to all of life's opportunities, not only the ones related to accumulating money.

Bronnie Ware, an Australian palliative care nurse, wrote a book called *The Top Five Regrets of the Dying* based on her years of working with people in their final days.

The people often said things they regretted weren't about wealth, status or achievements. One of the recurring sentiments can be summarised as: 'I thought life would start once things were sorted. It never occurred to me that this was it'.

Let that land for a moment.

They thought life would start once they had more money, got the promotion, bought the house, met the right partner, lost the weight or finally felt 'ready'.

But life doesn't start then because life is happening right now. The way you live your life day-to-day IS your life. It's not some far-off thing in the future that begins once you've checked all the boxes. This – right now, today, this moment – is it.

People often delay their own happiness until they have more money, but if you constantly say 'I'll be happy when', you are missing out on having beautiful experiences in life because you're not actively enjoying the now or creating your own joy. You are too busy convincing yourself you can't be happy until something external to you has shifted or been achieved.

Do you really think that you will suddenly learn to enjoy your life once you have all these big things?

No, because the goalpost is constantly moving. You've set yourself a new goal before you've had a chance to enjoy the one you've achieved now!

You have to make a conscious choice to create joy, have fun and celebrate your wins in the now *as* you work towards the bigger things you want in life.

If you keep waiting for life to start, you'll wake up one day and realise you missed it.

Remember: Your net worth won't be carved into your headstone. What will matter is the memories you made, how you enjoyed yourself and the way you connected with people.

When Fun Can Lead to Financial Growth

Having fun doesn't always have to be in the obvious, conventional sense.

When you feel stuck, lost or confused. . . whether it's 'how do I call in more money into my life?' or 'what career path should I take?', don't think that these questions ignore the rule of following your fun. . .

It is about doing what excites you the most in each moment – anything that has 'aliveness' or fun energy to it – in any capacity. Excitement is the thread to follow: Focus less on how it looks on the surface and more on how it feels. And over time, things will unfold naturally and you will create true wealth in all areas of your life, including financial wealth.

In growing my business, I noticed that the most financial success comes when I follow my excitement.

Previously, an idea would pop into my mind, but I'd write it down and wait for the 'right moment' to execute. I like to call my iPhone notes section the 'Idea Grave' because it's where exciting ideas went to die. With every week that passed that I didn't bring that creative idea to life, the less exciting it seemed to feel. It would lose its aliveness.

But when I act on an idea right away (within reason, and within my capabilities), allowing excitement to guide the way, magic would happen. My most successful digital course was launched within the space of two weeks from ideation to sales. My most fruitful brand partnership came from an excitement to follow up with someone I met at a networking event. My most viral video came from the excitement to share a story about my investing journey whilst on my morning walk.

Now, if you are not a content creator or business owner, you might think '*well how does this help me? I can't create my own income like you can*'.

Shanice Mears, who was just 21 years old, was working as an intern at Iris, one of the world's leading creative agencies. She followed the fun and excitement, and began sharing an internal newsletter about music, culture, fashion and other ideas that went round to the whole office. Not with any specific end goal in mind, she did it because it was fun. The former CEO, Dan Saxby, took notice, and their connection grew into mentorship and eventually a business partnership. Less than a year into her internship, guess what. . . the two of them (Shanice as an intern and Dan as the CEO) co-founded The Elephant Room – now an award-winning creative agency.

I share this story to remind you that you never know what you can create for your own future, but if you follow what feels fun, then it could lead you to magical ventures and exciting projects that change your entire life and financial wealth.

SOMATIC WORK

I love to dance – in my house, at festivals, in clubs or at gigs. If I hear a beat, you know I'll be moving and I don't care if I am being watched or not!

When you are dancing – really dancing, not self-consciously thinking about how you look but just moving and grooving – you're not ruminating on your financial stress. You are just listening to your body in the moment. And movement is a great way to get out of your head and into your body.

When I first started understanding the nature of the human experience, even with big insights that freed me immediately, I still had times when I struggled to 'get out of my head'. I still found myself caught up in thought spirals. And after reading this book, the same will happen for you too – and that's okay!

Somatic work can be very helpful when you feel like you are all up in your head. It is the practice of coming back into your body. Noticing what's happening physically – tightness, restlessness and shallow breath – and using movement, breath and sensation to reconnect with yourself.

When you're constantly in your head, everything can feel heavy. When you're in your body, it helps you get yourself out of your own mind.

Somatic work can be gentle or dynamic, and structured or intuitive. It might look like:

- EFT
- Dancing
- Breathwork
- Grounding practices (like feeling your feet on the floor or spending time barefoot outside)
- Strength training, walking or any form of exercise that brings you back into sensation
- Yoga – movement mixed with mindfulness

None of the above is a prescription, but merely something I wanted to share with you to do more of your own research if you feel called to do so. The power of somatic work allows you to drop back into your body when you feel overwhelmed, consumed by thought and struggling to see a way out.

PRIORITISING YOUR HEALTH

There is a saying that haunts me: **'People spend all their health getting wealthy and then spend all their wealth getting healthy again'.**

Let that sink in for a moment.

We're fed constant messages that success means sacrificing sleep, relationships, health and joy in pursuit of the next financial milestone. But what is the point of financial wealth if you destroy yourself in the process of building it?

Your physical health affects your mental clarity, which affects your financial decisions. Your stress levels affect your nervous system, impacting how you show up at work and your relationships. Your sleep affects your impulse control, impacting your spending choices. Your movement affects your mood, impacting your capacity to take aligned action.

It is impossible to separate your financial well-being from your overall well-being. They're woven together, each influencing the other in ways we don't even realise, until we start paying attention to our health.

Studies consistently show that poor mental health also makes it harder to make good decisions about money. When you're struggling mentally, your ability to manage, make and grow your finances is directly impacted.

Let me tell you about Polly, one of my first financial coaching clients:

She came to me because her business income had plateaued and her personal wealth was declining. She was a talented web designer, but kept under-charging, avoiding her business finances and turning down big opportunities. On paper, it could look like a pricing problem, imposter syndrome or a time management issue.

But I discovered that Polly was not prioritising her physical health, and it was having a detrimental impact on everything else. In an attempt to work as much as possible to make more money, she was sleeping 4–5 hours a night, skipping meals and hadn't moved her body properly in months as she remained glued to her desk. The brain fog was intense, and her mood was always low.

She was desperate for me to teach her how to change her relationship with money. Instead of giving Polly budgeting templates, pricing strategies or even a money mindset programme, I asked her to focus on something different.

The plan was simple: 7 hours of sleep, 30 minutes of movement and 30 minutes of nervous system care every single day. That was it.

Within a few weeks, she felt more focused, better rested and less anxious. And then naturally her financial reality began to shift.

- She had mental clarity to raise her rates
- She had the energy to show up at networking events, leading her to new connections and a new client
- She stopped saying yes to every project out of a fear of not having enough
- Her creativity returned, and she pitched a new service that immediately attracted new inquiries

This is not an either–or situation: Health and wealth can improve simultaneously, so if you believe that health and wealth are separate pursuits, please believe me when I say they are not. Taking care of your health from the get-go is one of the smartest decisions you can make. It will pay dividends and save your money in the long run too.

Your health protects your income: When you are burnt out, constantly stressed, sick or running on empty, your capacity to earn and create shrinks. Rest, movement, nourishing food and nervous system support are the very things that protect your money.

Poor health creates financial leaks: When your health is suffering, comfort and convenience can become part of your daily life – endless takeaways because you're too tired to cook, daily coffee because you are running on fumes and online shopping at midnight because you can't sleep. When your health is suffering, your financial habits reflect that, and those unintentional purchases or convenience buys all add up.

Caveat to this: I am not against takeaways, coffees or online shopping – I love all of these things! But there's a difference between *choosing* to get a takeaway and ordering one every night because you're too depleted to cook. There is a difference between buying something you love or need and spending money to fill a void or numb discomfort.

So, it is always good to check in with yourself, especially if you feel your financial habits aren't serving you or your financial situation is something you are struggling with and ask yourself:

1. When was the last time I had a full night's sleep?
2. Am I moving my body regularly?
3. Am I eating in a way that supports my energy?
4. Am I making space for rest and joy throughout my day?

True wealth includes waking up with energy, feeling at peace with your body, and having the mental clarity, health and vitality to actually live the life your money affords you.

It is impossible to enjoy your money if your mental, emotional or physical health is on its knees. Do not wait until you have reached your ideal destination of financial wealth to then take care of your health. **Taking care of yourself is the foundation for everything else – because health is wealth.**

SCHEDULE A MONEY DATE

One of the simplest ways to bring this embodiment into your finances is through what I call a *money date*.

A money date is intentional quality time with your money.

If we imagine ourselves as having a relationship with money, then money is the partner in this equation. I think we all know what a toxic relationship looks like? You don't know where the other person is, what they're doing, you ignore each other, spend no quality time together and the relationship is fractured with no real connection at all.

But a healthy relationship looks like the opposite. You want to spend time together, you know what each other is up to (in a relaxed, non-judgemental way), there is love, care and respect, and you have aligned goals!

This can be achieved with your money. So, let me walk you through how I do my money dates so that you can take what you need and create your own version:

1. **Set the vibe first:** I make myself a nice coffee or tea, light a candle, put on music I love or maybe sit outside if the weather is nice. I create an environment that feels calm and enjoyable and that I actually want to spend time in.

2. **Check in with my body first (if I am feeling anxious or overwhelmed):** Before I even open my banking app or my spreadsheet, I take a few deep breaths, feel my feet on the ground and remind myself that I'm safe.
3. **Review without judgement:** I look at what came in, what went out and where my money went. I check my financial goals and track my progress. I look at my investments and how they're performing. This is where your practice of noticing without observing comes in. Sometimes I spend more than my monthly budget, and sometimes I stick to my budget. It is all okay!
4. **Celebrate wins:** Did I stick to a spending intention I set? Did I save towards something that matters? Did I make a financial decision I'm proud of? I let myself feel good about it because financial wins always deserve to be celebrated.
5. **Get curious about patterns:** If I notice I overspent in a certain category, I get curious instead of critical. What was happening that week? Was I stressed? Avoiding something? Trying to soothe a feeling? What can I learn from this? Then, I set intentions for the next period so I can get more intentional.
6. **Close with gratitude:** I end my money date by acknowledging what I'm grateful for: the money I do have, the opportunities available to me, the progress I'm making and the abundance already in my life. It makes me feel all nice and gooey inside – what is not to love?

The whole 'date' takes maybe 30–60 minutes, and I usually do it monthly. It completely transformed my own finances from both an emotional and a practical point of view. And the same is true for every person in my community who has implemented this practice. You could try this out weekly, fortnightly or monthly – whatever feels good for you.

The point is to make it a regular practice, to create a relationship with your money that feels good instead of stressful and to actually get under the hood of what is going on with your money!

PART IV

Transforming Your Financial Journey

Chapter 17

Money as a Tool

Money is simply the tool: Choose wisely how you use it.

Money can be used as an incredible tool for life – not as a marker of success, not a source of identity and not the reason for your happiness, but something that supports you through all the seasons of your life.

There are two categories of people who have a good handle on using money as a tool to make more money: entrepreneurs and investors.

Entrepreneurs understand the power of using money to make more money by investing in their business to improve their cash flow. They sometimes utilise debt, in the form of business loans or funding, to turn an idea into a profitable business model and eventually pay back what they borrowed.

Investors understand that their money can make them money. When it comes to investing – whether it is in the stock market, in property or in other assets – they know that they are spending their money to use it as a tool to make *more* money.

Both are examples of pulling back the arrow to shoot it forwards again.

But money can be a tool for things *other* than making more money – a tool to have incredible experiences, make wonderful memories, build connections and support yourself.

- When has money supported you through something emotionally heavy or unexpected?
- How many memories, lessons and shifts in identity came from moments where you chose to *use* your money instead of clutching onto it?
- What opportunities has money created, even if they didn't feel 'financially smart' at the time?

I am not urging you to frivolously spend your money at every amazing opportunity you get because there will be an abundance of opportunities throughout your lifetime – I am sure of it. But knowing that money is and can be a tool for your life is such a beautiful reframe of money, and it is the very mindset that will help you find your wealth.

CHOOSING TO USE YOUR TOOLS

One example is the choice I made at the start of January 2026 – four weeks before the deadline of my final book manuscript – to fly to Bali to meet one of my best friends, Mary-Anne. As a digital nomad, she was travelling around the world and on many occasions had invited me to come and join her in different countries.

Even though I truly desired to live a more nomadic lifestyle, none of the chances felt right. But when she shared with me her plan to fly to Bali for the end of January and into February, before I even finished reading her message, I had started Googling flights for myself. Something about her invitation this time round, just felt right. . .

On paper, it didn't make financial sense – I was 'stretching myself' to be there. My savings were minimal (after they became my life-support during heartbreak). And business had understandably been slower during the months I had been writing – I knew that the 'quiet period' was actually giving me the space to focus on the book instead of being distracted by business deals but I was finally ready to increase my income and build up my savings again.

So, when this opportunity came along my wisdom knew what to do, even though my mind couldn't make sense of it.

Old Laura, the one who listened and acted in alignment with every negative thought that occurred about money, would have turned down the opportunity, ignored the nudges within herself and stayed at home, forcing herself through the writer's block she had been experiencing in December.

Instead, this new me trusted the whispers of my soul, and I knew it was right. No matter what, I would be okay.

I sent a message to my coach explaining the situation, and she sent back a playful but simple reply, '*It sounds like you have already made your mind up*', which brought me peace because she was right. I did not need to find ways to justify, validate, or explain why it felt right, it just did. And I trusted that feeling.

APPRECIATING YOUR TOOLS

I landed in Bali – a fresh country, the sun on my face and writing for 7–8 hours a day in that final week. We woke up and exercised. I ate healthy food. I got a good sleep. I meditated and journalled. I felt so unbelievably grateful to even have this opportunity. When I travel to new places, have adventures, experience new cultures, try new food... I feel truly wealthy.

Making content to share on my social media felt easy. Engagement was soaring, and my job felt fun and light. Words were flowing out of me so fast that I didn't once get stressed or think, '*fuck, I shouldn't be here*'. I felt excited about the prospect of finishing the book and getting back into the business to make more money and get my finances back on track. Ideas came to me randomly throughout the day that I acted on.

When I landed on the island, everything in me felt different. I felt abundant seeing all these other people living my idea of heaven, working in the sun, making money and living their best lives. I thought this could be me. . . then I felt, '*this IS me right now*'.

And then over the following days. . . magic occurred that reminded me how amazing it is to use money as a tool in your life:

First off, we were sitting in a coffee shop working and it was busy, so a random guy came and sat on our table with his coffee and pastry. The laidback energy of the place means everyone chats to each other so naturally we found ourselves in conversation about life and business. He had sold his business a few years back. . . He used to own a publishing company that published books from non-fiction experts. ARE YOU KIDDING ME!

We sat chatting for an hour, and he imparted all of his knowledge to me for free about best practices for marketing the book and promotion. What are the chances! I essentially got some free consultation with an independent book consultant who had the most amazing unbiased knowledge that gave me so many ideas for my book and my business.

And then, the day before the book was due, I had about 10,000 words left to write, but I was in the flow and feeling good. I wasn't caught up in any thinking, and I was utterly and completely in the present moment. . .

Then – BAM – an email landed in my inbox. It was confirmation from a client, unexpectedly securing a job for nearly £11,000 for when I return home.

This potential client followed me on Instagram, and after seeing my content in Bali, she sent me a message to pick the job back up. I am sure she had seen I was writing a book, saw the energy that was flowing through the screen and she was super excited to work with me, wanting to sign up for the full package I was offering.

Even when it didn't make much 'financial sense' to go to Bali, I listened to the nudges. I used money as a tool, knowing that I would always get something off the back of it. It created opportunities for me, connection with friends and new people. I felt present and like I was embodying a new version of myself, and the bonus of it making me money too.

How have you used money in the past as a tool for good, positive change in your life? How can your money support the version of you that you want to embody?

Because whether you're starting a business, healing from heartbreak, building a skill, travelling, resting or reinventing yourself, it is here to act as a tool.

Chapter 18

How You 'Make' Your Money

The source from which your money comes is an interesting topic to dive into. If you're employed with a stable income, it might seem like you're set up for that ideal, upward-sloping financial trajectory.

The perfect set-up: Regular pay raises, clearer financial planning and predictable savings can give the impression that your financial life should always be moving in a straight line.

You can set aside a portion of your income each month, make use of compound interest and build long-term wealth steadily.

But this mindset often ignores life's inevitable changes and creates fear around making big, soul-led decisions. For instance, what happens if you want to quit your high-paying job to follow a dream? Even if that job drains you daily, the perceived security it offers can keep you stuck.

FEAR vs. DREAMS

Let's say your dream is to leave your role as a lawyer to open a cosy coastal coffee shop.

It sounds beautiful, but it also requires stepping away from a job that looks good on paper – a job you've had for years and one that gives the illusion of safety. You might stay far longer than is right for you because you're clinging to the appearance of financial progress.

That fear of losing income or dipping into savings can push your dream further and further away. You ignore the nudges, suppress the excitement and close the door on a more meaningful life because you're afraid your net worth might dip.

Yes, chasing a dream might mean uncertainty and judgement from others, or take more time to reach your financial goals. You might use savings, face irregular income and feel wobbly at times.

But should that stop you? Absolutely not.

Imagine all the incredible businesses that would have been sent to the idea grave, where life-changing solutions, products and services never see the light of day – all because the person who had the idea was too scared not to follow the expected path of hoarding money to build wealth.

I honestly believe you are given your desires for a reason.

Seriously, if they're inside of you, they can be created in your reality.

Remember every single thing that exists in this material world was first invented in someone's mind. How fun it is to use our thoughts to create stuff, instead of believing fearful thoughts and causing our own suffering.

Not only this, but you would also be denying yourself the very life you truly long for – in this case, being self-employed. You know you were made for more than what you are doing, and you are finding courage to listen. You deserve to take risks and bet on yourself to manifest a peaceful, content life, unaffected by the trajectory of your finances.

But this rings true for the opposite case.

If you are a business owner right now, and there is a nudge inside of you to go back into employment, it is important you listen, explore it, and don't ignore your intuition.

So many people are scared to get a job because of what that looks like to others concerning their financial situation; yet, for many, it is the right next move. Perhaps you're in need of some extra financial support, and you know you can build up a reserve in employment for a period of time. Maybe you are tired of the entrepreneur life and are ready to relinquish some responsibility to be able to prioritise your health and well-being.

The very thing you need or want to do is the thing you are scared of. The fear of judgement from yourself or from people you know, friends, family and people online, freezes you into a state of avoidance and procrastination.

To be clear, this isn't a debate about employment vs. self-employment.

I don't think one is better than the other – genuinely. Both paths can lead to wealth and fulfilment, and both come with their own trade-offs.

Self-employment is often glamourised online. Yes, you gain freedom, deepen your self-awareness and can raise your income ceiling. But employment, when navigated intentionally, can be just as powerful. Many people build serious wealth by investing wisely while working 9–5.

THE FOUNDATION OF YOUR FULFILMENT

The real question is not how you make money or how much you make; it's how you *feel* about the way you earn it.

Not everyone wants to carry the pressure of generating their own income. Not everyone wants to build someone else's dream. And neither of those paths guarantees happiness. . .

I think if they did, the secret would be out, and we would all be jumping on board whichever option comes out on top.

In *Big Magic*, Elizabeth Gilbert shares the idea that '*it's okay to keep a job so your art doesn't carry the burden of paying the bills. In other words, you don't even have to love how you make money as long as that money supports a life filled with what you do love*'.

This is nuanced, but money should never be the foundation of our fulfilment. It can support it, guide it and even amplify it, but it should never be the source of it.

In Michael A. Singer's book *The Surrender Experiment*, he shares his experience throughout his life of entrepreneurship and making money. In his own words, he learned how to go with the flow through life even during the externally hard times. He was simply surrendering to life – not becoming a victim to his situation, even when objectively bad events happened. He remained open-minded to change, even when a path that felt so clear suddenly became a dead end.

His life is a series of wild, unexpected and incredible experiences. By releasing resistance to thoughts and impulses, he followed these inner practices of surrender, which led him from being a solitary yogi in the woods to unexpectedly building a multimillion-dollar business. In a life that was distinct from conventional employment, at times his life looked perfect to others while at other times his life was undesirable to most. Yet, he trusted his journey and allowed his inner compass to guide him through life without judgement.

It is so easy to look at someone successful and see all the riches and glory at the top of the hill, completely forgetting the financial challenges and obstacles that came along with it.

Singer's life was the embodiment of how money showed up as a natural consequence of surrender, not because he focused on acquiring it and hoarding it.

Whenever financial success came, he viewed it as life giving him the resources needed for the next step, not as something to attach to or chase.

Many people in Singer's shoes would struggle – clinging and clawing to an expectation of how they would want their life to unfold, such as the success of their business or the consistency of their financial progress. In doing so, many miss the opportunities to live a fulfilling and peaceful life, all because it didn't look exactly as they thought or it didn't fit the script they had written for their situation.

Learning how to be flexible, adaptable, present and open-minded is the source of your peace even in the midst of chaos.

The moment you let go of how you think life should be; you make space for how beautifully life can unfold.

Chapter 19

Embracing a New Financial Era

I would like to share a story with you about someone very special to me, a story that is deeply personal and close to my heart.

I know a woman who has not only lived the lessons in this book but has also fully transformed her life by embodying them.

She became a mother at a young age and spent years doing her best to raise her four children with the knowledge and financial resources she had at the time.

Across 10 years – the age gap between her eldest and her youngest – she took maternity leave but re-entered the workforce frequently, which had a huge impact on her capacity to make change. And like so many women, she felt the very real impact of the financial gender gap: the kind that leaves women with less in their pensions and fewer financial options later in life.

She was no exception.

She had to go back to work a lot sooner than she'd have liked, to bring in an extra income because a family of six was expensive. Sometimes she had to work during pregnancies, sometimes she took her young children to work with her, and for many years she had to lean on her eldest daughter for support with childcare and housework whilst she continued to supplement the household income. She always put her own happiness and health aside in an attempt to keep the wheels turning. And unfortunately, her employment was for survival, not for financial growth.

Once her children were all grown up, she decided she wanted more for herself. She didn't focus on the years she 'lost' or on her age, but instead looked to the future of possibilities with a positive outlook.

She began investing in her own financial education, tuning in to her inner wisdom and taking intentional steps towards a stronger, more empowered financial future. She believed in herself, no matter how long it took.

Over time, her income grew, debts were paid off and her savings account began to grow. She learnt how to invest, explored new opportunities, took calculated risks and had the courage and curiosity to pursue a range of side hustles, while trusting her own process and choosing to move when things felt right for her.

And then, sure enough, she reached a turning point. She stepped into the reality she had spent years quietly building, giving herself the option to walk away from a life that no longer served her.

At 63, she started a new chapter in her life, powered by her new financial stability and achieved through determination, patience and the elimination of judgement for herself.

That remarkable woman is my mum.

Her story is a beautiful and powerful reminder that:

1. **It is never too late to change your relationship with money:** No matter your age, your timeline or your past decisions, transformation is always possible when you choose to change your relationship to your thinking and money.
2. **Wealth is built first from within (through belief, courage and aligned action):** Your

financial growth is truly impacted when you change your mindset, trust your inner wisdom and take intentional steps even when the path is uncertain.

3. **Money is a tool for freedom, not a measure of worth:** Building your own wealth is never just about numbers. It is actually also about reclaiming choice, agency and the power to design a life that truly reflects you.

What struck me most throughout the process of writing this book is that money fears dissolve a little when you realise you're not broken, you're not behind and you don't have to figure it all out alone.

That's why I do this work – to remind you and myself that peace of mind and financial confidence can exist together; that you can create the life you desire, enjoy the journey, create your own true wealth and still grow your money; and that the growth of your money does not reflect who you are as a person. When you choose to loosen the power that money and your thinking have over you, everything can shift in an instant.

It was interesting that every time I shared the book with a friend or chatted to a person at the coffee shop about it, I would always have a beautiful and interesting conversation. Everyone has something to say about money. When I tell them what I do, everyone's response was '*Oh I could do with your help haha!*'. They have their own stories, beliefs and philosophies. They have their experiences and stories about the other people in their lives. Money touches everyone, and yet everyone has a different experience with it.

Every person said to me: '*Wow I cannot wait to read this book*', which reminded me how pertinent financial struggles are around the world. And if you are one of those people, I am glad this book made its way into your hands.

I hope that if you have found your way to this final page, you feel lighter, more hopeful and excited about what your financial future holds. I hope you trust in your ability to create a new financial reality, and that money becomes a fun, playful and abundant resource for you as you find your own version of wealth.

Acknowledgements

To Alice and Gemma, my publishers at Wiley, thank you for believing in me as an author long before I believed in myself. And thank you to Kelly and Sherri-Anne, my editors, for making my life so easy and upholding the vision of this book and what I wanted to share with the world. And to everyone else on the team at Wiley, thank you!

To my family: Mum, you are truly one of the kindest, most generous and positive people I have ever had the privilege of knowing, and I am so grateful for your constant support. I know that no matter what path I take, career I choose or person I become, you will be cheering me on, so thank you. To my little sister, Beth, and my two brothers, James and Andrew, thank you for always keeping me grounded, testing my patience and reminding me how proud you are of me. I love you all.

A special mention to someone who is littered throughout the book – my phenomenal coach, mentor and friend Jessie. Thank you for every story shared, every question asked and every call and voice note. I am so grateful to be in this conversation with you – for encouraging me to share my truth and for supporting my journey. You have left an incredible mark on my life. For me, peace of mind is no longer a myth but, in fact, a reality.

When I attended the first retreat you co-hosted with the amazing Wyn Morgan (thank you, Wyn, for having such a beautiful impact on my life), I could never have imagined the beauty that would unfold. I remember hanging out with you and Jo on that final evening after it ended, and I felt like *nothing had changed, but everything was different*. Jo and I went on an emotional and spiritual roller coaster for weeks afterwards, questioning everything about our existence as we knew it. . . And the place I have now landed is home, in the present moment. Thank you for the work you do.

To Troll and Worm, you've witnessed me at my highest and lowest moments over the last few years (endless nights spent chatting and listening to me in my pink dressing gown). You were there when my heart broke wide open, and you were there when this book became real. Thank you for being such a huge part of my growth.

And to 'The Womb', my sanctuary – to Triple J – the laughs we have all shared will be forever etched into my heart (and my abs), long live our home.

To Fran and Beth, from our English A-Level class where I nearly failed (Miss Jewitt will be so proud!) to our little home in London – the place where this new version of my life was born. You encouraged every new step I took, and our time together in Bermondsey shaped so much of my life that has followed. Thank you both so much for your never-ending support. VVH forever.

To Mary-Anne, our time in Bali will hold a special place in my heart! I am so grateful for you and our long-distance phone calls (always passing the baton). Thank you for your endless support.

To every single one of my beautiful best friends: I could write an entire chapter about each and every one of you and how you have individually impacted my life for the better. You have seen me through all the different chapters of my life and of this book, and I am forever grateful for all the support, the laughs, the love and the impact you have in my life – Char, Em, and JJ, Nina, Big Elo and Little Elo (SDP), Gabs, Sarah and Jenna, Lydia, Carly, Emma, and Sarah. To me, female friendship is true wealth.

To ALL of my FinFluencer friends, I am lucky to be in the most beautiful and supportive community. Everyone I have met, spend time with, lean on, co-work with, and chat in the financial education space. Thank you for cheering me on every step of the way, for inspiring me and always allowing me to be myself (there are too many of you to name, but you know who you are). And to my gorgeous VA, Sarah, for supporting me in my business and laughing at my jokes.

Thank you to the coffee shops I adore – to Fuckoffee in Bermondsey where my business turned from a side hustle to a full-time business, to ButterUp Coffee in Tulse Hill for always making me the best cups of cacao for my morning creative walks, and to The Hill in Streatham (formerly known as SW16 Bar & Kitchen) for keeping me caffeinated and fuelled while I wrote this book.

To Kieron: The decade I worked with you shaped the woman I am today. You have been one of my most significant male role models in my life, and I am grateful for the day I spelt both of your names wrong on my job application. Thank you for always believing in me and pushing me to be better.

Thank you to my previous therapist, Kate. During my quarter-life crisis, you made me feel comfortable sharing things that I have never even admitted to myself. It may have been many years ago, but our sessions helped me find a new sense of hope for my future.

To my ex, the Frenchman, I loved what we shared. Our ending broke me at the time, but I am so grateful for my transformation that followed. You taught me so much about myself and showed me what was possible. C'est fou.

My most important thank you goes to you, the reader, for spending your finite time with me across these pages in pursuit of feeling better about money. This book is dedicated to each and every one of you who are called to live life differently and experience money in a new, fresh way, which ultimately will lead you to having the wealthiest life you could ask for.

About the Author

Laura Moore is a Financial Well-Being Speaker, Creator and Educator, Certified Financial Coach, and Money Mindset Expert on a mission to change the way people think, feel and talk about money. Known for her fun and jargon- and judgement-free approach to financial education, Laura has built a reputation as one of the United Kingdom's most trusted and relatable voices in the personal finance space, with a growing online community across all social platforms.

She is also the host of the *Mind Money Soul* podcast, with episodes dedicated to exploring the emotional, practical and spiritual sides of money, reflecting her belief that true financial transformation goes far deeper than just numbers and spreadsheets.

After saving over £40,000 by the age of 27, Laura began sharing her financial journey online and found herself on *BBC News London* sharing savings tips with over six million people who tuned in, and she hasn't looked back since. She was named in *The Times* Top Rated Financial Advisers and Coaches list for both 2023 and 2024, nominated for the British Bank Awards' Online Financial Influencer of the Year three consecutive times – in 2022, 2023 and 2024 – and was honoured as one of *Brummell Magazine*'s Inspirational Women: The Champions in 2025. She has been featured across leading publications including the *Financial Times, The Times, The Telegraph* and *FT Adviser.*

Her interest in personal development and psychology led her to complete her Financial Coaching training in 2022, and she has since worked with a wide range of clients on a one-to-one basis, helping them identify and shift the financial behaviours, beliefs and patterns that were keeping them stuck.

Beyond her media presence, Laura delivers financial well-being and money mindset workshops, panels and keynote talks for some of the world's leading organisations, including Amazon, TikTok and EY, and Elemis, and is passionate about creating a more inclusive financial landscape – particularly for women who are ready to rewrite their money story and create a life of abundance and true wealth.

Laura has also been actively involved in advocating for systemic change in financial education at a policy level, participating in discussions facilitated by GoHenry with Members of Parliament at both the House of Commons and the House of Lords as part of efforts to introduce financial education into the UK school curriculum.